WHAT'S
YOUR
F★CKING
SIGN?

WHAT'S YOUR F★CKING SIGN?

Sweary Astrology for You & Me

AMELIA WOOD

CASTLE POINT BOOKS
NEW YORK

www.castlepointbooks.com

The Castle Point Books trademark is owned by Castle Point Publishing, LLC.
Castle Point books are published and distributed by St. Martin's Press.

ISBN 978-1-250-27228-7 (paper over board)
ISBN 978-1-250-27248-5 (ebook)

Design by Tara Long
Edited by Monica Sweeney
Special thanks to Jennifer Calvert

Our books may be purchased in bulk for promotional, educational, or business
use. Please contact your local bookseller or the Macmillan Corporate and
Premium Sales Department at 1-800-221-7945, extension 5442, or by email
at MacmillanSpecialMarkets@macmillan.com.

First Edition: 2020

10 9 8 7 6 5 4 3 2 1

CONTENTS

UNLOCK THE SECRETS OF THE FUCKING STARS 1

UNLOCK THE SECRETS OF THE FUCKING STARS

How much easier would your life be if you had insider info on what makes people tick? Wouldn't you feel better knowing that your coworker keeps dropping the ball because they're a scatterbrained Sagittarius and not because they live to piss you off? Or that your brother's so fucking chill all the time because he's an even-tempered Libra?

I know—it sounds crazy. But this shit is magic. Knowing a person's zodiac sign really can give you the edge in understanding how to deal with the people in your life. How do you get Taurus to spice things up in bed? Respect for prep time. When should you approach your Cancerian boss with your big idea? When you have doughnuts. Why can't Gemini make a fucking decision? Blame their hamster. Astrology has an answer for everything.

Keep in mind that a person's sun sign is just the tip of the informational iceberg. A lot depends on not just their birthday, but also their time of birth *down to the fucking minute*. If you can get that kind of info from your boss/friend/date without sounding like a fucking psychopath, more power to you. In the meantime, just start here.

What's Your F*cking Sign? helps you find the best ways to relate to your managers, coworkers, love interests, friends, and family by spilling all the tea on their astrological makeup. Screw your skepticism—just give it a read. You'll be amazed at how helpful this shit is.

ARIES
One Fiery Motherfucker

AKA
The Ram

BIRTHDAY
March 21–April 19

SIGNS
Fire | Cardinal | Masculine

RULED BY
Mars

ON A GOOD DAY
Passionate, Fearless, Independent

ON A BAD DAY
Impulsive, Selfish, Stubborn

FAMOUSLY ARIES
Vincent van Gogh, Chance the Rapper, Lady Gaga

The first thing you have to know about Aries is that they have zero chill—but that's not a bad thing. The adventurous go-getters born under this sign win gold medals, start businesses, take to the streets for good causes, and generally get amazing shit done. They also can't sit still for two consecutive fucking minutes, have no patience for speed bumps, and refuse to lose (and if they do, it's not done gracefully). That means that you can often find these fearless folks barreling headfirst into the unknown like cartoon rams with anger-management issues. But, armed with the right info, you can help bring out the best in Aries, and their best is pretty fucking incredible.

ARIES

THAT 9-TO-5 GRIND WITH ARIES

WORKING UNDER ARIES

Aries isn't just a boss. Aries is *the* boss. The phrase "fearless leader" has never applied to any sign more than this one. Aries are just built for it. (And they fucking know it.) Aries bosses are crystal clear about what they want, never second-guessing their course. And because they're so damn capable and optimistic, you can't help but fall into line behind them. That energy is intoxicating! Sure, their expectations can run a little high. (Like, Snoop Dog high.) But they can also be passionate and magnanimous bosses that make going to work pretty fucking exciting.

How to bring them your brilliant ideas

This sign is all about challenging the norm and creating change. But with so many bold ideas of their own and no time to waste, Aries isn't here for your long-ass PowerPoint presentations. When you've got something to say, get straight to the fucking point. Drop the bomb, ask for the raise, make your argument, and stand your damn ground. Aries bosses respect courage, so show them that inner badass. And don't be discouraged if they lose their shit. They just need a minute to adjust to the notion that not all great ideas originate with them.

How to show them your A game

With Aries, sucking up will get you nowhere. (Thank God. Who wants to be *that* guy?) Instead, the best way to impress an Aries boss is to be just as fearless and dynamic as they are. When they come up with a new initiative—which will be every other damn day, because their beautiful mind is always at work— make big plays. When you have an idea, come at them with the mic drop and be ready to back up its worth (succinctly). Aries is all about the hustle, and they respect the hell out of independent thinkers like them. But it can't hurt if you happen to make them look good while you're at it.

How to keep it real

You know how Wile E. Coyote is so focused on killing the Roadrunner that he ends up flattened by his own Acme-brand anvil? Yeah, Aries feels that. Eternal optimism combined with intense focus can make these folks a little shortsighted, so you need to be their eyes (and sense of fucking reason). When you see Aries going off the rails, avoid bruising their ego. Fix things on the DL or take your boss aside to have a quick and quiet chat. With Aries, you have to pick your battles and find ways to give them a win. (Oh, and never, ever get in their face. It will not end well for you.)

ARIES IN THE TRENCHES WITH YOU

Teaming up with Aries? Get ready to feel unstoppable! Whether they're giving the orders or executing them, Aries is a fucking force to be reckoned with. And that confidence is delightfully contagious. But rolling with Aries means riding shotgun—these natural-born leaders need to be in the driver's seat if they're going to do the impossible (which is always their M.O.). Show them they can count on you, and you'll get along just fine.

How to get great shit done together

Aries needs a Goose to their Maverick—someone as fearless as they are who will play to their strengths and balance out their weaknesses. This is the sign of big ideas and bigger egos, so let Aries take the lead now and then. (And try to keep your cool when they start bossing you around. They can't help their astrological DNA.) Together, you can save the day and crush those quarterly projections! But for the times you can't, get the pom-poms ready. Aries isn't great with defeat, so your boy will need some bolstering to get back in the game.

HOW AN ARIES BOSS FIRES YOU

You: I'm just not feeling as though our office environment is open to new ideas and opinions.

Aries: You're right. No one should feel uncomfortable in their environment. I'd encourage you to find a job in another one.

You: No, I just mean—

Aries: Best of luck!

How to become work besties

When it comes to Aries, you don't get a second chance at a first impression. They either like you or they don't, and good luck working with them if they don't! (No pressure.) Want to get on their good side? Just be straight with them. Aries is wary of suck-ups and players. They want to know you're on the level, and that means being honest and direct from the get-go. So if you're going to stroke their ego—and you should—you're going to have to summon some sincerity.

How to send out an SOS

If you want the help of an Aries, all you have to do is ask. Despite a distinct lack of touchy-feely vibes, this sign loves to be needed. But think of Aries as more Batman and less Dear Abby. They make an enthusiastic hero in a pinch but resent being called on too often. Plus, they turn into the world's crankiest grandma when asked for advice—zero filter, lots of opinions, and a healthy helping of guilt if you don't take what's offered.

THE ARIES EMPLOYEE

If Aries was born to be the boss, then they'll make a garbage employee. Right? Wrong. Given the right opportunities and encouragement, people born under this sign make enthusiastic, innovative, and exceptionally driven workers. They'll gladly take direction and follow the rules while bringing their starry-eyed optimism to the drawing board when you need it. But this is Aries we're talking about, so yeah, you'll need to rein them in now and again. And "detail-oriented" is not on their résumé—just save yourself some trouble and foist the mundane shit onto the nearest Virgo.

How to get them motivated

You'll find this sign lacking plenty of beneficial qualities (humility, patience, and self-preservation instincts come to mind), but motivation isn't one of them. Aries doesn't need Tony Robbins. Aries *is* Tony Robbins. (If Tony weren't a Pisces.) Just point your Aries employee in the direction you want them to go, and then get the hell out of their way! And if you really want to gas them up, give them challenges to tackle, opportunities to lead, and words of encouragement. But don't overload them—although Aries employees seem invincible, they can break down when overwhelmed.

How to light a fire under their ass

Anyone—even an Aries employee—can hit a slump. But this sign literally is fire, so you won't need the explosives to get their ass moving again. What these hardcore badasses really want is a little coddling. No, seriously. Aries employees need to feel valued and accomplished, but they spend half their time trying to do the impossible and plowing into brick walls. Occasionally, you'll need to tend to their wounded confidence and throw some smaller, more doable shit into the mix. Make Aries feel needed, and the rebound will make your head spin.

How to have the hard convos

This is the one area where being direct with Aries won't help you. While Aries is happy to dish out the criticism, they sure as hell can't take it. This sign is wired to succeed. Failure is not an option. Blame is for other, lesser people. When breaking bad news, you have to warm Aries up to the idea that they aren't the perfect creatures they see in their ego-addled minds. Start with subtle hints that something's up. (But don't nag. Aries hate being nagged.) Then, bring the funny. Laughter helps the medicine go down.

ARIES

LOVE,
SEX, AND
FOR-EV-ER
WITH
ARIES

THE ARIES MEET-CUTE

Look for the person doing victory laps around the pool table or dartboard at any bar, and odds are good that you've found an Aries. Does that sort of swagger appeal to you? Good. Because you're in for a lot of it when you start hanging out with someone born under this sign. Subtlety is not Aries's strong suit, but at least you'll know when you've caught their interest. And once you do, these passionate extroverts will charm the fucking pants off you (literally). If you can keep up, you're in for the adventure of a lifetime!

How to woo the shit out of them

These natural-born leaders tend to do the wooing, so all you really have to do is get out of their fucking way. Let Aries show off, stroke their ego, and be ready for anything. But most importantly, do you. Not only does Aries love a challenge, but they also respect the hell out of an independent spirit. So show Aries that you have your own shit going on and let them enjoy the thrill of the chase, then give them your undivided attention when they catch you. Knowing that you want them but don't need them is everything.

How to dazzle on your date

If your Aries is planning the date, you'll need to check your introversion at the door. In case you haven't noticed, candlelit dinners aren't really this sign's style. (Zero chill, remember?) If you're in the driver's seat, you want to challenge your date, show them something new, or get their body moving. Preferably all three. Think: axe throwing followed by Brazilian churrascaria (the kind where the waiters walk around with giant sticks of meat and feed you until you want to die). Either way, be bold! And put your fucking phone down—Aries needs all the attention.

How to cut through the bullshit

Sure, this sign loves to put on a show. But that Aries ego isn't bluster—it's optimism and energy. When it comes to bullshit, they actually have a zero-tolerance policy. Aries values honesty and sincerity above all else. (They're also not tactful enough to bullshit anyone.) The flip side of that endearing quality is that they have opinions stronger than a Long Island iced tea. But they don't expect you to hold your tongue. Part of keeping up with Aries is showing them that you can handle a verbal sparring match with wit and grace. So bring it!

BETWEEN THE SHEETS WITH ARIES

Ever stay with someone who drives you crazy because the sex was just that fucking good? Yep, probably an Aries. This fire sign was built for stellar sex, and they're here for it whenever, wherever, and however they can get it. After all, sex has everything Aries loves: action, passion, creativity, fun, and plenty of incentive to cross the finish line. That competitive drive can lead to some rather quick victories, but they'll be ready for the next match in no time. And luckily for their longtime partners, that fire never burns out. (Hugh Hefner was an Aries. Just sayin'.)

How to whet their appetite

Think of Aries like a gas stove with the pilot light constantly burning—it doesn't take a lot to crank that shit up to high heat. But you can skip the wine and rose petals; most of Aries's turn-ons lie outside the bedroom. No, that doesn't mean adventurous balcony sex. (OK, that doesn't *just* mean balcony sex.) It means they prefer intellectual foreplay. Spend the day challenging each other, and Aries will be raring to go when you get home. If you want Aries to stick around long term, though, you've got to make them work for it for a while.

BREAKING UP WITH ARIES

Aries during a breakup:
[Lists everything you've ever done wrong and a few things that weren't even you.]

Aries after a breakup:
U up?

How to blow their fucking minds

Being with an Aries is all about giving as good as you get—in lighthearted competition, during battles of wit, and, of course, in the bedroom. Those first two often lead to the third. With Aries, there's less makeup sex and more mid-fight sex. So be impulsive, show your partner you're ready to play, and encourage creativity. Most importantly, don't be shy! Aries has no patience for modesty. Or for lingerie with laces and hooks. (Go with the snaps.) And remember: Aries approaches sex with the same vigor that they approach everything else, so limber up and stay hydrated!

How to get what you need

This is where the Aries ego works to your advantage—they want to know they're the best you've ever had. That means that getting what you want is as easy as asking for it. At least, *during*. Aries is not the shag-and-snuggle type, so if you ask them to spoon afterward, they may die a little inside. They'd rather connect with you over leftover Chinese food in the kitchen. One word of caution: If you're the monogamous type, you should pump the brakes and have a conversation. Aries tend to spread the love around, but they're also up front about it.

WITH ARIES FOR THE LONG HAUL

The fact that Aries is always chasing shiny objects like a human magpie might give you pause about getting into a relationship with one. That's fair. But however flirtatious and self-centered they can be, Aries are also loyal and supportive partners who will always be up front with you *and* have your back. This sign has that "knight in shining armor" shit down pat. As long as you're honest, sensitive to their feelings, and thick-skinned with yours, your life together will always be filled with laughter, excitement, and achievement. Not to mention mind-blowing sex.

How to have a great fucking partnership

Members of the Aries clan aren't looking for a yin to their yang—they're looking for someone who can keep the hell up. That doesn't mean they don't *need* a little balance. Having an adventurous, independent spirit is obviously a must, but you should also be more even-tempered than your human fuse of a partner. When they start to blow up, wave the white flag or walk away and let them cool off. Let them know that you don't respond to yelling or insults and help them find better ways to communicate. And know that any fight will be short-lived—Aries are physically incapable of holding a grudge.

How to deal with the day-to-day shit

Although Aries love to call the shots, they're more than happy to heap all of the household responsibilities onto their partner. Sure, you could argue about it. But with Aries's temper, you're better off splitting the chores with a cleaning service. (Just make sure it's in the budget—Aries's impulse buys can lead to trouble in that department.) You could also make their ego and natural problem-solving inclinations work to your advantage by reframing chores as challenges. But like the smart, beautiful, high-energy border collies they basically are, they'll need praise or a reward for any efforts.

How to ensure you'll be a cute-AF old couple

You'll never find yourself relaxing in rocking chairs with an Aries, but that makes growing old together even better. Devoted, encouraging, protective—this sign is your ride or die. It's the two of you against the world. Tell Aries your goals, and they'll make sure you reach them. They'll also call you out on your shit when you need it most. But that knight in shining armor instinct is serious, so don't offer up any problem you don't want solved. Let Aries fix what they can, and forgive them when they start tilting at windmills. (And if you just want to vent, call a Pisces.)

ARIES

IN THE CIRCLE OF TRUST WITH ARIES

ARIES IN YOUR SQUAD

When it comes to Aries, you've got a friend for life. Sure, you might see a friend-shaped blur more often than not. But when they find time for you (between work and rugby tournaments and last-minute backpacking trips to Costa Rica), you'll have their undivided attention. If you need a quick fix, short emails are the way to go. But Aries are always there when you really need them, especially if it involves fucking up someone who's wronged you. And it only takes a few minutes with them to make you feel invincible and help you get your shit together.

How to have a fucking blast together

Having a good time with Aries will never be a problem—that's what this sign is all about. Just make sure you have your passport, all of your shots, plenty of caffeine in your system, and a good fucking attitude (no downers allowed). They may have to squeeze you into their jam-packed schedules, but people born under this sign don't waste a fucking minute of time with friends. And they'll probably have a few interesting ideas about how to spend it. Just remember, these guys don't give much thought to money, so you'll have to.

How to get the tea

How do you get Aries to tell you what's on their mind? Be breathing near them. This sign gives out opinions like they're handing out free skin care samples at the mall. But getting Aries to talk about themselves is a whole other thing. They need to know they can count on you and that you respect them. Being honest, supportive, and trustworthy is a start. Bonding over your mutual hatred of whiny pop icons can also help. But asking for their (obviously brilliant) insight when you have a problem will have them spilling the tea in no time.

How to make things right

One of the many wonderful things about befriending an Aries is that you'll know immediately if you've pissed them off. There's no, "Gee, I hope I didn't offend them." By the time you're wondering that, they're either icing you out or losing their shit. If it's the former, wave the white flag and apologize. There's room for only one stubborn asshole in this relationship, so it can't be you. If it's the latter, let them get it off their chest. Once they do, it's like it never existed. Either way, you'll be back to hitting the trampoline park together in no time.

ARIES IN THE FAMILY

Bottom line: life with an Aries will always be more fun than life without one. And when they're family, they're far less likely to ghost your ass. But an Aries is an Aries, and any relationship with one will need a foundation of honesty and respect, not to mention a good fucking amount of compromise. You'll never be able to change that fiery temperament or get them to admit they're wrong, so you may as well embrace the passion and courage that keeps life interesting!

How to have an awesome relationship with an Aries parent

Aries's "work hard, play hard" philosophy can get this sign into some pickles when it comes to parenting. They often blur the line between parent and pal, making it tricky for kids to figure out which is which. And when an Aries parent feels disrespected, that fiery temper ignites. Even when you're a grown-ass adult, in order to keep the peace it's best to avoid challenging an Aries parent's authority. But Aries make it easy to forgive any short-lived blow-ups and appreciate the optimism and encouragement that make you feel like Charlie being handed the keys to the chocolate factory.

A FEW OF ARIES'S FAVORITE THINGS

* Doing shit they were warned not to do

* Punching shit and then getting mad that it hurt

* Turning everything into a competition

* Saying whatever pops into their heads

* Jumping into new relationships with people who pay them literally any attention at all

ARIES

How to raise a kick-ass Aries kid

People born under this sign never really grow up, which means Aries kids are exactly like Aries adults—energetic, optimistic, stubborn, and confident. Give Aries kids room to grow and learn but also boundaries, shower them with plenty of attention, maybe teach them first aid, and baby-proof your house (this shit starts young). The trick to parenting this sign is to encourage their brightness and creativity by channeling that crazy energy into something constructive before you lose your fucking mind. More than anything, just be there for them. Gentle, consistent support is everything.

How to go from siblings to BFFs

Having an Aries sibling can feel like having an extra parent—these guys take the lead from day one. But beneath that bravado, Aries can feel like an outsider in their own family. Making your sibling feel needed, included, and supported will go a long way in smoothing over any distance or rifts. And once you get past the pushiness, you get to soak up all of that infectious optimism and become their partner in crime. So instead of fighting for rank, let Aries lead you, teach you, and drag you into crazy adventures. Life will be a hell of a lot more fun!

THE LAST WORD

So, now you know that Aries is basically a headstrong, high-energy human shot of cinnamon whiskey. But you also know that being around an Aries can help you go harder, love deeper, and get. shit. done. As long as you're straight with folks born under this fiery sign (and don't mind participating in the occasional MMA fight), you can have one hell of a relationship.

Aries Motto

SORRY, NOT SORRY

TAURUS
Steady AF

AKA
The Bull

BIRTHDAY
April 20–May 20

SIGNS
Earth | Fixed | Feminine

RULED BY
Venus

ON A GOOD DAY
Loyal, Supportive,
Romantic

ON A BAD DAY
Materialistic, Lazy,
Inflexible

FAMOUSLY TAURUS
Queen Elizabeth II,
Cher, Dwayne
"The Rock" Johnson

You can always count on a Taurean, mostly because people born under this sign *really* hate change. These stalwart (OK, stubborn) folks have deep wells of patience and perseverance, making them your go-to guys when you need to get shit done. But don't expect Taureans to burn the midnight oil. These charming tastemakers consider self-care a religion, so you'd have to drag their comfy, sweatpants-clad asses out from under their cozy, chunky-knit throws. You'll probably never beat 'em (because Taureans refuse to lose a fucking argument), but joining them is more fun anyway.

TAURUS

THAT 9-TO-5 GRIND WITH TAURUS

WORKING UNDER TAURUS

Taureans are all about that corner office, and it's not just because they believe they're the only ones who can get the fucking job done. For these luxe-loving folks, money really does buy happiness—in the forms of swanky goods, cozy furnishings, and five-star pad Thai. That's why Taureans are likely to lock down that secure paycheck rather than venture into the unknown. Luckily, they aren't into micromanaging (yay), but they will test your ass when you least expect it, so don't get too comfy. As bosses go, though, you could certainly do worse than one that's predictably logical and clear about their expectations.

How to bring them your brilliant ideas

First things first in getting your Taurean boss on board: leave that sloppy shit at home. Whether they're the CEO or an unpaid intern, people born under this sign have zero patience for incompetence. So get your shit together, schedule a time to talk, and then make a strong, data-backed case for what you want. Taureans love a good informational handout, too, but they're not here for your hype. Just keep the vibe cool and profesh. And whatever you do, avoid making idle threats if things don't go your way. Taureans don't play.

How to show them your A game

Want to impress a Taurean? Keep your head down and do your fucking work. These dedicated folks won't be swayed by you jumping through hoops for them. They just want to see that you can get shit done. And if you can show them that you have both a plan and a backup plan, all the better. Anticipating any potential questions they may have or problems that might arise is huge for these employers. So is taking responsibility for your work—the buck has to stop with you if you're going to earn your boss's respect. But bringing gourmet doughnuts to work never hurt, either.

How to keep it real

Once you've shown your boss that you're someone they can count on, you shouldn't have any trouble getting along. But Gucci help you if you have to deliver bad news—literally. Appeal to Taurus's desire for comfort and indulgence. You know how injuries are always worse if you expect them and tense up? That's Taurus when facing any sort of surprise. So ease them into the conversation, calmly present the facts, and suggest a solution (don't go in there without a fucking solution). Then encourage your boss to enjoy a long lunch and some retail therapy.

TAURUS IN THE TRENCHES WITH YOU

Having a Taurus on your team means that shit will always get done. And life will be a lot fucking easier for you if you can let go and let Gary (assuming Gary is a Taurus). Those born under this sign are not only hardworking and dependable, but they're also super-thoughtful and efficient. And they know it, so be prepared for them to dig in their heels if someone challenges their obviously flawless logic. If that someone is you, make your case calmly and back it up with data. As long as Gary gets the final say, he'll be happy to hear you out.

How to get great shit done together

If Taurus had a coat of arms, it would read: "If you want something done right, do it your-fucking-self." These folks hate wasted efforts, and they don't put up with bullshit or ineptitude. But when everything really does fall on them, they can feel exploited and pump the brakes. Show the Taureans on your team some love and help them find balance. For example, let them create the PowerPoints while you add the finishing touches and the feels. Just keep an eye on the budget—Taureans are good with details but a little spendy with the company card.

TOP 5 REASONS TAURUS CALLS OUT OF WORK

1. Wine-and-cheese hangover
2. It's cold outside
3. The latest season of *The Crown* came out
4. They know the breakroom is out of Cap'n Crunch
5. They're exhausted from doing everyone else's work

How to become work besties

You won't catch a Taurus brown-bagging it or working through lunch if they don't absolutely fucking have to, so getting on their good side can be as simple as asking them to grab lunch. They'll be thrilled to have a self-care buddy to spend some breaks with. (Just don't expect them to be on time for those breaks. Like, ever.) At work, show them that you trust their judgment and avoid butting heads. Taureans may seem bossy as fuck sometimes, but it's only because they've thought things through to a disturbingly detailed degree.

How to send out an SOS

You won't find a better comrade-in-arms than a Taurus. Because Taureans think that their way is always the best way, they're more than happy to dole out the advice. And this kindhearted sign is super-generous with time and resources. Just don't be tempted to take advantage of that—Taureans have a strong reaction to anyone being used or mistreated, themselves included. They'll play the role of the hero if they have to, but these natural-born peacemakers would rather coach you from the corner than fight your battles. Either way, they can help you work shit out.

THE TAURUS EMPLOYEE

Considering that Taureans live to be the boss, you might think that they'd make super-annoying employees. But these ambitious professionals know they won't make that scented-candle money by getting under their boss's skin. Instead, they work their asses off to become indispensable. But Taurean employees aren't without their faults—namely procrastination, that signature stubborn streak, and a physical inability to be on fucking time. All you need is the right kind of honey to motivate these worker bees, and you'll see some serious results.

How to get them motivated

When a Taurus is in the mood to work, there's no fucking stopping them. And rallying that persevering spirit is pretty simple: be clear with your expectations, then get out of your Taurus's way. Because Taureans are thorough as fuck, you'll probably need to answer more than a few questions and quell any doubts. But if you show Taureans you trust them with the task, they'll want to do you proud. And when they do, make sure you let them know how much you appreciate the hard work. A little bit of gratitude goes a long way.

How to light a fire under their ass

When clear expectations aren't enough, it's time to break out the big guns—perks. Appeal to Taurus's "work hard, relax hard" vibe by dangling a comfort carrot. Anything from catered lunches to performance bonuses will do the trick. And although they're not much for the spotlight, they do love them some prestige. An encouraging word from the Big Boss will kick Taurus's shit into high gear. If all else fails, an honest critique might be all you need. Just remember: Taureans don't respond well to being pushed, so stick with gentle nudges.

How to have the hard convos

Notice that the symbol for Taurus is a bull? Yeah, that doesn't bode well for you when telling a Taurus something they don't want to hear. You're basically that guy with the fancy hat holding the red flag. And like that guy, you have to be bold and just fucking get on with it. Your weapon: the facts. (You come at tenacious Taureans with feelings at your own risk.) They may put up a fight, but if you're calm, clear, and logical, you should be able to walk away with a mutual understanding and all of your limbs.

TAURUS

LOVE, SEX, AND FOR-EV-ER WITH TAURUS

THE TAURUS MEET-CUTE

You might not be able to put your finger on it, but there's something instantly appealing about a Taurus. Sure, they're usually pretty cute. And when they're not wearing sweats and becoming one with their fucking couch, they rock some nice threads. But it's more than that. This sign is ruled by the planet Venus, meaning Taureans are hardwired for romance. That doesn't mean you won't have to work for their affection, but these fiercely loyal partners love with their whole hearts. So don't even go there if you're not ready to go all in.

How to woo the shit out of them

Ready to shoot your shot with a Taurus? Tread lightly. If you want to get anywhere with this sign, you have to let them take the lead. They need to set the pace and feel things out in their own time. Taureans ~~like~~ *need* to weigh their options, so giving them the time and space to think things through will win you major brownie points. While you're at it, let them do the talking (aside from complimenting their impeccable taste). Taureans love a quiet confidence. Make them wonder what the hell you're about and they'll be compelled to uncover more.

How to dazzle on your date

If a Taurus has agreed to relinquish control for a night (hey, it could happen), suggest taking a walk around the botanical gardens or trying the hot new restaurant in town. Despite the fundamentally different vibes, sensual Taurus will love either option. Food, nature, and comfort are top three on their wish list. That last one is especially important— keep things low-key and make sure your date is physically and emotionally comfortable with everything that's happening. If they don't feel secure, no amount of (admittedly delicious) fucking pasta will get you a second date.

TAURUS

How to cut through the bullshit

This one's easy: Taureans don't do bullshit. (Or flings. Too much change, not enough comfy pants.) If they like you, you'll fucking know it. They keep it 100 at all times—as in, they are 100 percent invested from the moment they realize they're into you. So if you're going to date someone born under this faithful and enduring sign, you need to cut through your own bullshit. Get really clear on what you want before you bring Taurus into it, and make sure you communicate every step of the way once you do.

BETWEEN THE SHEETS WITH TAURUS

If you're looking for someone to work through the *Kama Sutra* page by page with you, you might want to pick up a Pisces. Taureans are not known for their adventurous sexcapades. In fact, their love of routine and hatred of surprises extends all the way to the bedroom. Some might call sex with Taurus "vanilla," but that doesn't mean that it's boring. Super-sensual Taureans can make you weak in the knees with their touch and wear you out with orgasmic all-nighters. Quickies may not be in their repertoire, but foreplay definitely is.

How to whet their appetite

They're certainly not the spontaneous type, but make no mistake, Taureans fucking love sex. They just need a little time to prepare (shower, shave, pick an outfit, light some candles, take a power nap). Make Taurus's need for advance notice work to your advantage by sending sexy texts throughout the day to rev them up. Let them know how much you want them. And when you're together, focus on touch, which is super-important to sensual Taurus. Try removing items of clothing one at a time and gently caressing or massaging each newly exposed area.

ASKING TAURUS FOR A SECOND DATE

You: Had a great time tonight. Wanna try this again sometime?

Taurus: ...

You: Maybe next week?

Taurus: Hang on. I'm working on my pro/con list.

TAURUS

How to blow their fucking minds

Like good food and yoga pants, sex is a treat for Taurus's senses. Play into that by appealing to all five. Break out the sexy underwear, put on some mood music, and start things off with a nice massage (paying special attention to the ears and neck, which are Taurus's fave erogenous zones). Scent is a huge turn-on for this sign, so light some scented candles and make sure you smell good enough to eat. Speaking of which, food play is the one area where Taureans don't mind things getting a little messy. Honey, strawberries, whipped cream—go crazy!

How to get what you need

Once Taurus gets comfortable with a particular sequence of events, shall we say, it'll be tricky to shake things up. But don't fret—it can be done. Just communicate clearly and calmly the things you want to try, then give Taurus time and space to get used to the idea. Avoid trying to switch things up mid-tryst if you don't want your fucking ego bruised by your partner's "deer in the headlights" face. Unless you're just so exhausted from marathon sex that you need an out. But suggesting a snack break is less likely to result in an existential crisis.

WITH TAURUS FOR THE LONG HAUL

Snuggling up on the couch to stream movies and eat takeout night after night? Taurus was built for this shit. Not only do relationships appeal to this sign's love of routine (and inability to handle change like a normal fucking person), but they also play to the strengths imbued in the sign's ruling planet. Taureans are nurturing, caring, steady, and loving companions. Sure, they can get a little possessive. And yeah, they may need a bit more reassurance and affection than most. But these charming partners will always give as good as they get.

How to have a great fucking partnership

The best partnerships are built on mutual respect and compromise, right? It might seem like an uphill battle with bull-headed Taurus, but compromise is possible—you just have to speak this sign's language. Present your case clearly, calmly, and without letting your emotions (i.e., fury) run away with you. The last thing you want to do is get into a pissing contest with Taurus, who will argue with you until they're blue in the fucking face. Instead of locking horns, show Taurus that you understand where they're coming from. That's all they really want.

How to deal with the day-to-day shit

Unless you give zero fucks about your living space, plan on having the same fights about it on replay. Taureans are very particular about the things they surround themselves with and how they're arranged. On one hand, you benefit from Taurus's high-end taste (and the work ethic that pays for it). On the other, you might have to go to the mat for the things that matter to you. Give your Taurus a little time to get used to your ideas and they should come around. But don't think you can just sneak in a few things from TJ Maxx without them noticing.

How to ensure you'll be a cute-AF old couple

The real trick with Taurus is to not get bogged down in the details—they'll do enough of that for both of you. Try to bring balance to the relationship, kicking your partner's ass when they get too comfy and helping them let go when they're in high gear. And make sure you keep the romance alive—if Taurus's needs for sex and affection aren't met, they may start to stray. And despite the double standard, your eye should not wander for the fucking duration. Super-possessive Taurus may forgive, but they never forget.

IN THE CIRCLE OF TRUST WITH TAURUS

TAURUS IN YOUR SQUAD

Taureans might make tricky bosses and stubborn mates, but they make kick-ass friends. This sign will always have your back, be there to hold your hair and put your ass in an Uber, and give you the real talk you need (whether you like it or not). And as the king of common sense and objectivity, Taurus's advice is top-notch. Plus, they're protective, warm, genuine, and caring, like the older sibling you wish you had. Whether you're hanging on the couch or heading out for midnight sushi, you can't beat time with a Taurus.

How to have a fucking blast together

Gee, however could you have fun with someone who spends all their free time shopping, eating delicious fucking food, getting pampered, and chilling in their super-comfy home? Sounds terrible, right? It might be if you don't like shopping—they take that shit seriously. But otherwise, it's pretty damn easy to enjoy your time with a Taurus. Just don't expect them to show up on time for their own carefully devised plans. Taureans mean well, but their brains are usually on overload. (Hence the need for massive amounts of self-care and rest.)

How to get the tea

Taureans are pretty damn picky about who they let into their inner circle, so count yourself lucky if you're one of the chosen few. But if you want a Taurus to open up, you still gotta earn it. This stalwart sign is always there for you when shit gets crazy, and they'd take torture over letting one of your secrets slip (even if it was just a drunken hookup that nobody but you fucking cares about). Taureans show up for you, and they expect you to show up for them. That's the only way to earn their trust.

How to make things right

If you fuck things up with a Taurus, you'll know it. This straightforward sign does not suffer fools. They'll probably forgive the little shit, magnanimous friends that they are, but don't think for a second that they'll forget. Fuck up one too many times, and Taurus will ghost your ungrateful ass. And it'll break their faithful heart to do it, so channel Taurus's multitrack mind and think shit through before you act. And when you do fuck up, take responsibility for your actions. The only way out of the mess you created is through.

TAURUS IN THE FAMILY

Patient, nurturing, affectionate, protective—these are definitely qualities you want in a family member, and Taureans have each one in spades. Of course, they might also hold you to some pretty high standards. But that really seems like more of family thing and less of a sun-sign-specific thing. At the end of the day, Taureans just want the best for the people they love. They'll defend you, support you, and adore you. And they'll feed you. A lot. All you really need to do is learn to live with that fucking stubborn streak (a small price to pay).

How to have an awesome relationship with a Taurus parent

Taurus parents are the kind you see in sitcoms. They're the ones who "help" their kid create an A+ solar system when the kid clearly didn't need or want their fucking help. But they're also the ones who listen affectionately, dole out the warm hugs, and fill their kid's lunch box with Twinkies and encouraging notes. And when that kid grows up, empty nest syndrome comes along to kick them in the ass. So go easy on your Taurus parent. Let them feed you and feel needed, and forgive them for acting like Marine One when you were a kid.

PLANS WITH TAURUS

@You: snowboarding this weekend?

@Taurus: hard pass

@Taurus: Netflix and nap?

How to raise a kick-ass Taurus kid

Taurus kids are the fucking best. Their need to succeed has yet to eclipse their love of food, music, and art, so they're just freely creative. And they have plenty of friends to kill time with. But they may occasionally need you to light a fire under their lazy ass. More than that, they need to learn how to express their anger so that it doesn't build up and boil over. Let them know that it's OK to be angry, then give them the coping mechanisms this generous sign needs to deal with shitty friends for years to come.

How to go from siblings to BFFs

Whether your Taurus sibling is older or younger, whether you like them or not, they're your natural-born guardian, the enemy of your enemies. They're as stubborn in their support of you as they are in their opinions. So when they're bugging the shit out of you, remember that it's nice to have someone in your corner. Sure, Taurus siblings may be a little blunt. And yeah, yours probably outed you for breaking shit when you were little. But it's time to be the bigger person. Instead of butting heads over every little thing, just let your protector be right.

THE LAST WORD

Ready to make Taurus love you? Whether you're in a boardroom or a bar, the advice is the same. Arm yourself with facts, gratitude, scented candles, and Thai food, and you're basically a damn shoo-in for that raise. Or date. Or bromance. And because Taureans are the living embodiment of self-care Saturday, it's a good bet that making them happy will make you happy, too!

Taurus Motto

NAMASTAY IN BED

GEMINI

The Ultimate Smartass

AKA
The Twins

BIRTHDAY
May 21–June 20

SIGNS
Air | Mutable | Masculine

RULED BY
Mercury

ON A GOOD DAY
Adaptable,
Compassionate,
Communicative

ON A BAD DAY
Insecure, Flaky,
Superficial

FAMOUSLY GEMINI
Ralph Waldo Emerson,
Marilyn Monroe,
Kanye West

Don't be fooled by this sign's reputation for superficiality—Gemini's thirst for knowledge and razor-sharp wit are no fucking joke. And that flakiness everyone gossips about? It's just amped-up adaptability. These super-capable folks can do anything they put their minds to, and they're always on the hunt for their next challenge. Prone to people pleasing, Geminis often use their chameleon-like talents to become whoever you need them to be. But when people born under this sign are true to themselves, they're kickass employees, passionate partners, loyal friends, and a bright light in the darkness.

GEMINI

THAT 9-TO-5 GRIND WITH GEMINI

WORKING UNDER GEMINI

You might mistake Gemini's occasional bossiness for a desire to be the boss, but this sign's really not about climbing that corporate ladder. Don't get it twisted—they're super-smart badasses who can totally run a company if they want to. But they'd much rather be part of a team, which is why you'll usually find your Gemini boss in a coworker's cubicle instead of their big, shiny office. They're also amazing at delegating and trusting their team to handle shit on their own. And that's really for the best, because Geminis can't make a decision to save their fucking lives. (Their hamster never stops running.)

How to bring them your brilliant ideas

Geminis love a new idea with a fresh perspective, so don't think twice about offering yours up. They probably pop by your office to say hi once a day anyway, so finding time to talk won't be an issue. You won't have to bother with any sort of presentation (which will just bore the crap out of them anyway), but you do have to have your facts straight. Gemini is quick to catch on, but they always have a million questions. That annoying indecision of theirs? It actually stems from trying to gather and process every fucking piece of information in existence.

How to show them your A game

Gemini bosses love an employee who's bright-eyed and bushy tailed and wants to talk "big picture" with them, but they *need* someone who can handle the damn details without bugging them. If they give you the ball, run with it. If you bring them a problem, have at least two possible solutions in hand. Show Gemini that you're on top of your shit by anticipating their questions and having the answers at the ready. And most importantly, *never* bring down the office vibe. A positive, collaborative work environment is everything to Gemini, who maintains a 24-hour creative buzz.

How to keep it real

When you have a Gemini for a boss, flexibility is key. You gotta be ready to roll with whatever crazy, brilliant, exhausting thing comes out of their mouth next. These folks change their minds like they change their underwear (possibly more often), so you can always expect them to throw a fucking wrench into your perfectly planned project. When you want to bring them back to the pack, appeal to their insatiable curiosity—throw out a few breadcrumbs and have them "help you" figure things out. They'll see your idea in a whole new light.

GEMINI IN THE TRENCHES WITH YOU

These multitasking masters can help you get a handle on any project. Not only are they incredibly flexible, great under pressure, and awesome at offering fresh perspectives, but they're also just fun to be around. Geminis love to make people happy. Sometimes that means bringing in cookies for everyone (homemade, of course); other times it means busting out a stand-up-style rant about the IT department. Oh, and they're handy AF. Broken copier? Not a problem. In fact, they're thrilled to do anything that breaks up the day. If they're forced into a routine, you can expect a rant about that, too.

How to get great shit done together

If you're working with Gemini, you're pretty much guaranteed to get great shit done together. This sign was born to be the yin to someone else's yang. (Literally. Gemini's symbol is twins.) With a mind that travels a million miles a minute and natural charm, Geminis can help you devise and sell any grand plan. But at some point, you're going to need to cut them off from doing any more research, which they consume like Jell-O shots at a frat party. Geminis feel like they can never know enough to make an informed decision.

ONE HOUR AT WORK WITH GEMINI

Boss: Can you compile a marketing plan for this?
Gemini: On your desk!

Coworker: Do you know how to convert this to a PDF?
Gemini: No problem!

Maintenance Guy: Help me patch this drywall?
Gemini: I'll get my putty knife!

GEMINI

How to become work besties

Geminis get along with everyone. In fact, you'd have a harder time *not* being their work bestie. They're just a good time—they love to laugh, have an adventurous spirit, and can riff like your own personal Amy Schumer (also a Gemini, obvs). And they're happy to be your go-to guy or gal for work issues and life advice alike. But this sign can *talk*, so steer clear of their cubicle if you need to get shit done. (It's easier than cutting them off, which is one of the only ways to offend them.)

How to send out an SOS

These mental meanderers will do anything to get away from their life-force-draining desk. But Gemini's favorite distraction is helping a coworker in need, so all you have to do is ask. Or look confused anywhere near them. Or swear loudly at your computer. They're basically Daredevil, swooping into action whenever they sense trouble. But if you seek out their help or advice, you better at least give it a go. Geminis hate wasting their efforts on someone who won't listen to fucking reason (which, according to them, is anything that comes out of their mouths).

THE GEMINI EMPLOYEE

Geminis are the utility players every team needs. These high-energy employees think on their feet, love a challenge, and can get more done in a fucking hour than any other sign in a day. They just need a creative, forward-thinking work environment where they feel free to share their gifts. Natural-born helpers, Geminis care more about fulfillment than money (good news for you!). But undervalue them at your own risk—this sign knows its worth. And as marvelous multitaskers who crave variety like it's chocolate, Geminis always have a side hustle they can bounce to.

How to get them motivated

Presenting Gemini with a challenge is usually motivation enough—they're puzzle-loving nerds and compulsive problem solvers. Get clear on the results you want so that you can answer any questions Gemini has. And they will have questions. If Gemini doesn't see the "why" behind what they're doing, good fucking luck getting them to do it. But once they understand your logic, they're off to the races! Boredom, on the other hand, is their kryptonite, so leave the monotonous crap for the Cancers in the office.

How to light a fire under their ass

When you need Gemini to stop procrastinating (which they do because they know any task will take them half the fucking time it takes anyone else), it's time to appeal to their ego. Folks born under this sign know how good they are, and they need you to know it, too. Show them that you trust them with the big shit. Tell them how much you appreciate their efforts. Mention the times you've been impressed with their results. And if that doesn't work, offer to buy them the latest Mac Pro—shiny new tech revs their engines.

How to have the hard convos

Shocking as it may be, Geminis don't love criticism. (But really, who does?) They take that shit personally. And that makes it a battle to get them to accept responsibility for their actions. So try to keep things upbeat. Instead of tearing them down, turn that criticism into a challenge. If you absolutely have to get into it with them, prepare for a debate—and the possibility of losing. Gemini won't let go of something that doesn't make sense to them, and they can be disturbingly persuasive.

LOVE, SEX, AND FOR-EV-ER WITH GEMINI

THE GEMINI MEET-CUTE

Charming, smart, flirtatious, funny—it's like Geminis were built for this dating shit. This multi-passionate sign loves a little of everything (and too much of nothing), so you're just as likely to find them in a bookstore as a bar. Or at a park. Or befriending the produce guy at the grocery store. Striking up a conversation with Gemini isn't the hard part; keeping up with them is. But it's well worth trying. Time spent with this sign can give you a whole new lease on life!

How to woo the shit out of them

Conversation is Gemini's currency, so other air signs will have an automatic in. But don't despair if you're an earth sign! Opposites can still attract if you bring a good sense of humor and a little curiosity to the table. Got some witty banter in your back pocket? Even better. Geminis love to laugh and make others happy, so playful repartee lets them know you get them. And that's the most important thing! Geminis need to feel appreciated and seen. The quickest way to fuck things up? Let your attention wander while they're talking.

How to dazzle on your date

Geminis will try anything once. They'll also crack jokes the entire time, so you might want to skip the movies. Go to something new together so you can talk about it, or go for the immersive experience. (Do you know how much fucking fun it is to do an escape room with a Gemini? They'll have you laughing so hard you can't see the damn clues, but they'll still get you out in record time.) Better yet, let them pick the place. There are few things Geminis enjoy more than introducing people to new things to love.

How to cut through the bullshit

Geminis may be a lot of things—usually all at once—but they're never boring! They are, however, tricky to get to know because they're busy being who you want them to be. (Except if you want them to be someone who remembers the plans you made. In fact, you might want to help them set up their calendar app.) These master communicators could use a little help feeling comfortable and letting their guard down. And although they put up a good front, overanalyzing can leave them with some serious self-doubt. So just be patient and kind.

BETWEEN THE SHEETS WITH GEMINI

Let's see…allergic to routine, wants to make others happy, has a good sense of humor, insatiable curiosity, and one hell of a mouth. Where else could these attributes come in handy? You guessed it! Geminis are awesome in bed. Not only do these enthusiastic lovers get off on getting you off, but they also use their gift of gab to do it. Dirty talk and sexting are squarely in Gemini's wheelhouse. And because they're used to transforming themselves into other people, so is role-playing. So basically, sex with Gemini never gets old.

How to whet their appetite

Everything you do with Gemini starts with great conversation, including sex. Playful banter, witty barbs, deep insights—it's all foreplay to a Gemini. That and some really imaginative dirty talk. And when you want to shut them up, a damn good kiss will do the trick. But Gemini also loves to see a little effort and appreciation. Surprising them with some new lingerie, a home-cooked gourmet meal, or even a weekend getaway will pay dividends in the bedroom. They'll hold on to those good feelings for a lot longer than one night!

GEMINI'S TOP 3 PASTIMES

1. Stalking their friends' exes on social to get the tea

2. Fact-checking someone and proving them wrong

3. Turning all the shit they've been through into jokes

GEMINI

How to blow their fucking minds

Luckily for you, it's pretty fucking easy to please Gemini because they enjoy all things a little more than the next sign, and sex is no exception. If you want to go the extra mile, make sure you keep things interesting with new moves, positions, and places. Your job is to keep them out of their own head so they don't overthink it (like they do everything else). And try to keep up, because Geminis are down for anything and their creativity is next level. Whatever you want to try, Gemini is here for it.

How to get what you need

Sex is easy; it's intimacy that's hard. But even hinting at what you need should be enough to get Gemini's attention. This sign is great at reading people, even when they're a little... distracted. Of course, there's always the option of asking for what you want. No sign is more open to suggestion and experimentation than this one—it's exactly what they need to stave off the boredom of routine (which is death for a Gemini's libido). Plus, their people-pleasing tendencies come with a kickback in the bedroom—turning you on turns them on. So, get yours!

WITH GEMINI FOR THE LONG HAUL

Geminis bounce through life like Tigger heading for a picnic. Although it can take a minute for this sign to settle down, they make faithful companions when they do. (Shameless flirts, but faithful companions nonetheless.) Any unpredictability they bring to a relationship is well worth the love, strength, positivity, and inspiration they bring with it. A relationship with Gemini means bouncing through life together. This sign still loves their independence, but that makes sharing experiences with them that much sweeter. Gemini doesn't *need* you, they *want* you. And they'll spend their boundless energy making sure you know it.

How to have a great fucking partnership

Geminis are easy to love and hard to live with. They can be moody and flaky, they're constantly going off on tangents, and they will rip you to fucking shreds in one breath if you come at them. But they're also incredibly thoughtful, great at anticipating your needs, and always ready to pull you out of the darkness with some laughter and light. So be patient with Gemini. Understand that any flakiness is just a symptom of the ultimate ping-ponging going on in their head. And make sure you're always honest with them—Geminis can smell bullshit coming, and their forgiveness is hard-won.

How to deal with the day-to-day shit

For Gemini, chores are the epitome of all things boring and monotonous as fuck. They'll kick their procrastination into high gear to get out of doing dishes or laundry. (Unless they can put on some *Parks and Rec* while doing it. Multitasking the annoying shit with fun shit is the only way they'll find the motivation.) The one exception might be organizing, which lets them tap into their creative problem-solving skills. And expect them to rearrange the furniture at least once a week. They can't stand shit sitting in one place for too long.

How to ensure you'll be a cute-AF old couple

Say it with me: "Yes, dear." Why would you even try to argue with this sign of silver-tongued devils? When they're wrong, they'll never admit it. And they'll probably gaslight you into apologizing. So for your own fucking sanity, pick your battles. This is a marathon, not a sprint. Once they find a partner who's a match intellectually, energetically, and physically, they're loyal for life. Help your Gemini feel appreciated and understood, and encourage that fiery, independent spirit of theirs. The trade-off is a sense of wonder that keeps you both young!

IN THE CIRCLE OF TRUST WITH GEMINI

GEMINI IN YOUR SQUAD

Geminis get a bad rap for being shitty, two-faced friends. But don't let a few gossipy bitches spoil the bunch. Most Geminis are genuine, loyal, loving people who just want to see their friends happy. And they'll do anything they can to make that happen, whether it's delivering monologues like a late-night host to make a friend laugh or giving sage advice in times of trouble. Forever searching for their other half, they find a little bit of a twin in everyone and let that part of their personality shine. Gemini might even understand you better than you understand yourself.

How to have a fucking blast together

When Geminis find a "twin" (i.e., kindred spirit, or maybe just someone who feels the same way they do about raw tomatoes) they feel whole—which means they just don't fucking understand alone time. They're down to do literally anything if they have a bestie by their side. Why eat, travel, or work by yourself when you can do it with a friend? Luckily for you, they have lots of "besties" to hang with. God knows you're going to need some downtime after a day full of adventure, mischief, and gut-busting laughter with Gemini.

How to get the tea

Gemini's reputation for gossipmongering is well earned—they know how to spill some damn tea. But when they do, it's usually because they believe they can trust you with it. Unsurprisingly, that doesn't always work out for them. And if they've been burned in the past, you can bet they'll learn from it and be extra guarded in the future. Show them the love and support they need to open up to you. And maybe ask for their help doing something physical, like cleaning out your closet. Knowing Gemini, a little tea might turn into a martini-infused fashion show.

GEMINI

40

How to make things right

For as much as they talk, Geminis keep most of their real feelings bottled up to avoid burdening anyone. They may come off as cool and unaffected, but this sign is actually pretty selfless and sacrificing. And they assume that others are, too. So when friends abuse their trust or take advantage, it feels like it came out of the blue and hurts that much more. Prepare yourself for some serious saltiness—when you hurt a Gemini, they hit back. And don't even think about pulling the same shit twice. That'll be the end of the friendship.

GEMINI IN THE FAMILY

Some signs feel like they can only be their true selves around family. Gemini is not one of those signs. In fact, they may take the chameleon game up a notch to avoid disappointing family. (Their immediate family, anyway. They can usually take or leave their extended family, minus that cousin who's more like a friend.) They love their family so much that they work that much harder to please them. And because that's exhausting, they may not be very reliable for Sunday suppers. But they're always there when their family needs them.

How to have an awesome relationship with a Gemini parent

Geminis make some amazing parents, especially for extroverted kids. To them, children are just more friends to inspire. (Sorry, introverts, you're going to have to forgive them for constantly pushing you out of your comfort zone. You can't argue with the results.) They love to live vicariously through their children, watching them grow, explore, and experience life. And they take it *hard* if their kids push them away or ignore them. So make sure you take an interest in the things they show you. One day, you'll appreciate the sense of wonder they instilled in you. ★

HOW TO WIN A BET WITH GEMINI

You: I'll bet you $10 you can't keep your mouth shut for 5 minutes.

Gemini: Hey, I don't have to talk . . .

You: So, Sarah texted her ex last night.

Gemini: YOU HAVE TO BE FUCKING KIDDING ME! Oh, screw you. Just take your damn money.

How to raise a kick-ass Gemini kid

You know those videos of cats knocking shit off tables? That's what happens when brains meet boredom, and you can expect the same from a Gemini kid. It'll be your job to help keep them engaged in a positive way. That is, if you don't want them fucking up your shit. Encourage your Gemini's natural curiosity, creativity, and independence by letting them explore, tinker, and talk. But balance that out with structure. They need to learn self-control and focus so they don't grow into scatterbrained adults. Don't smother their wild spirit, just be there to guide it.

How to go from siblings to BFFs

Geminis live for their siblings. Need some money? A kidney? It's yours. They're happy to share. This sign has a "you and me against the world" attitude with their brothers and sisters. After all, siblings are the first people to fill the "twin" void, the ones who make Gemini realize how much more fun it is to share experiences with others. That's why they'll work their ass off to mend any rift. And if they can't, they'll spend their life trying to fill the void with friends… and possibly cats. So. Many. Cats.

THE LAST WORD

Life with a Gemini is never boring, but at least now you know why. And really, that's half the battle. So, next time their indecision is driving you up a fucking wall or they won't stop talking, you can be ready with the wit and wisdom they need to quiet that damn hamster. Be Gemini's sounding board, let them know it's OK to be real with you, and you'll have a fun-loving friend for life.

Gemini Motto

OK,
BUT
WHY?

CANCER
A Human Bullet Journal

AKA
The Crab

BIRTHDAY
June 21–July 22

SIGNS
Water | Cardinal | Feminine

RULED BY
The Moon

ON A GOOD DAY
Brave, Nurturing,
Passionate

ON A BAD DAY
Stubborn, Selfish,
Passive-Aggressive

FAMOUSLY CANCER
Ariana Grande,
Princess Diana,
Meryl Streep

If you're lucky enough to have a Cancerian in your life, you know what it's like to be loved, understood, and protected. The kind and sensitive people born under this sign feel everything deeply and lean into comfort and security (for both themselves and those they care about, which is nearly everyone). But don't let that fool you—this cardinal sign knows how to take control. And they can be downright vindictive when fucked with. Get to know this sign better and you'll see only the best in them!

CANCER

THAT 9-TO-5 GRIND WITH CANCER

WORKING UNDER CANCER

Like Aries, Cancerians are natural-born leaders. Unlike Aries, they try not to be a dick about it. Cancerians know that they can be a little *particular*, maybe even a bit demanding at times. But they also know that they have to keep their team happy if they want to be successful. Their hard-ass tendencies come from a fundamental need for shit to run smoothly—this sign *cannot* handle chaos. Or dustups. Or, well, speed bumps. So although they're happy to have a discussion about how things are run, they don't have any patience for people challenging their authority.

How to bring them your brilliant ideas

Cancerians make supportive, fair-minded bosses, and they really do want to hear their team's awesome ideas. But because they constantly operate on empathy overload, the emotional part of their brain usually kicks in before the logical part. Translation: they get triggered easily. So, try to catch them in a good mood and watch for any signs that you're starting to piss them off (at which point, you switch fucking tack immediately). If your appeal is mindful of their needs and thoroughly outlines all of the important points, you shouldn't have a problem.

How to show them your A game

No need to jump through fiery hoops for your Cancerian boss. These folks are on top of their shit— they see you. And they've got a running tally in their head of all the times you've come through (and all the times you've complained about the thermostat). If you really want to impress a Cancer, be someone they can count on. That means doing the work, but also learning how to read your boss. This sign's superpower is anticipating people's needs, and all they really want is for someone to do the same for them.

How to keep it real

Cancer is known for being home to some moody bitches (blame the Moon), so you may find yourself having to manage up now and then. Try to catch your boss at their most relaxed (which might mean buying their assistant a drink every so often so they'll give you a heads-up about what you're walking into). Then show up with solutions, not problems. And if you have to light a fire under their reluctant ass, show them you have both a consensus and a deadline. Also, bring doughnuts. Sometimes it's not the Moon. Sometimes they're just fucking hangry.

CANCER IN THE TRENCHES WITH YOU

Not only do Cancerians generally kick ass in the work realm, but they're also warm, loyal team members. This sign's spirit of "We're in this together" will help motivate everyone involved to do their best work. But don't think you can take advantage of their efforts or goodwill. Offend a Cancerian and they will ice your ass out. (Let's just see you try to get anything done without them.) One more tip: go easy on the interruptions. These folks are focused as hell and will jump out of their fucking skin if they don't see you coming.

How to get great shit done together

Getting shit done with a Cancer isn't hard—this sign does not quit. And they have a knack for knowing everyone's strengths and assigning tasks accordingly. In fact, Cancerians are so good at reading people that they don't understand that it's not a common skill. If it's not one of yours, make sure you ask your Cancerian coworker what they think, and often. They won't offer up that info because they assume you already know, but their ideas can be the difference between *good* and *garbage*.

HOW CANCER HANDLES A NEW BOSS

What they think: Hmm... How can I make you feel important enough to do what I want you to do to and run this company the way I think it needs to be run? Hope you're as easy to handle as my last manager.

What they say: Coffee, boss?

How to become work besties

Cancerians are experts at keeping their work and personal shit separate, so if you want them to blur the line, you have to earn it. That means being someone who takes work seriously—they have zero patience for people who make their jobs harder. You'll also need to learn how not to step on their emotional toes. (Get on their bad side and you're likely to stay there, though they'd never let that interfere with their work.) But if you really need a shoulder to cry on, a Cancerian will always be there for you.

How to send out an SOS

Because Cancerians feel personally responsible for every fucking thing, they're not super quick to give advice. They also tend to suffer from imposter syndrome, which makes this very capable sign think that their advice is crap. But it's not, and they want to help. They're dying to help. They might just take a little convincing. And maybe a promise that you won't hate them if shit goes south anyway. But they're happy do whatever they can for you. The best approach? Give them a little time and advance notice to think things through thoroughly.

THE CANCER EMPLOYEE

There's a reason you see so many Cancerians climb the corporate ladder (two, in fact): they're really fucking good at their jobs and they're loyal as hell to their companies. People born under this sign are quick to take the lead and tackle extra responsibilities. They're also born for desk work—give them all the spreadsheets and leave them the hell alone. And if you can drag their keen observations out of them, your company will be all the better for it. Want to keep them happy? Foster a work culture of stability, community, and consistency.

How to get them motivated

Cancerians are the workhorses of the zodiac, so you can bet they're pretty damn self-motivated. But if you want them to do their best work, tell them why it's important. Understanding and believing in their contribution appeals to their empathetic personality and gives them a foundation that they can fall back on if their motivation begins to slip. You'll also need to address any concerns that they have. And if they tell you they're not cut out for a certain job, believe them. They're not blowing smoke up your ass— they're being honest.

How to light a fire under their ass

Getting a Cancerian to move quickly is like trying to make paint dry faster. What they really need are optimal conditions, and even then, the increase is marginal. This sign is not big on change or sudden movements. They need prep time. And if you push them too hard, they could end up fighting you every step of the way. So do not poke the passive-aggressive bear. Instead, let the bear pick its own fucking tasks. Cancerians are the best judges of their capabilities anyway, and they won't want to let you down.

How to have the hard convos

If you know you have a tough conversation with a Cancerian ahead of you, just get the hell on with it. This is a sign full of empaths. The longer you wait to deliver the blow—even if you're trying to soften it— the more they can feel it coming and tie themselves in fucking knots about it. So put these soft-hearted folks out of their misery. And do it with kindness— Cancerians will blame themselves for any poor outcome, even if they had no control over it. The less personal the critique, the better.

LOVE, SEX, AND FOR-EV-ER WITH CANCER

THE CANCER MEET-CUTE

Cancerians tend to be introverts and homebodies, but they know how to break out the charm when they need to. This super-observant sign probably saw you coming and decided whether they liked you by the time you said "Hello." If they caught you showing off, your chances of a date just went down in flames. But if you can prove that you, too, are an empathetic observer, you might have a shot. (Hippie-ass Aquarians need not apply.) Just know that, while Cancerians can fuck around, they're more likely to want a relationship.

How to woo the shit out of them

When you meet up with a Cancerian, start taking mental notes immediately. (Convert these to text later. You'll want to refer back to them.) This sign is most impressed by someone who knows them inside and out—their likes, dislikes, childhood memories, upcoming doctor's appointments…. People who can remember *all* the personal details are their kind of people. And since most of us can't, we have to write that shit down and set reminders. Other than that, just keep things low-key and give your Cancerian time to figure out who you are and how they feel about it.

How to dazzle on your date

Cancerian opinions are like cement—they set quickly and for life. People born under this stoic sign know what they fucking like, and what they don't. Make life easy on yourself and let them choose the setting for your date. You might end up in the corner booth at a quiet restaurant or heading for a walk on the beach. Any which way, you just want to show them you trust their judgment implicitly. Whatever you do, don't try to convince them to try something they've said they don't like. They will drop your ass so hard your fucking tailbone will break.

How to cut through the bullshit

The only bullshit you'll catch from a Cancerian is a by-product of self-doubt—they make up for a lack of confidence with an extra helping of humility. This sign prizes honesty as much as they do empathy. They also know themselves well enough to express how they really feel. But thanks to that natural intuition, they'll know when *you're* trying to hide shit. So just don't. Cancerians catch feelings fast, and they run deep. The only way to avoid hurting them is to be up front about what you want.

BETWEEN THE SHEETS WITH CANCER

Although Cancerians love to lead in the boardroom, they'd really rather *not* in the bedroom. Don't take their reluctance to initiate as an indication of performance—this sign can bring the fucking heat. They'd just rather let go and enjoy, which is something they can't do anywhere else in life. Keep in mind that Cancerians only give as good as they get, so your shit had better be on point, too. If they do end up unsatisfied after being overly generous, they'll resent the hell out of you.

How to whet their appetite

Time to break out those old-school seduction techniques! Cancerians can be oddly old-fashioned when it comes to sex—they prefer to keep things private, and the sex will always be hotter if they're in a loving relationship. When it comes to foreplay, it's all about romance. Take the time to set a proper mood with candles, caressing, and plenty of kissing before you move on to other things. (The fact that their astrological symbol looks like the number 69 is no coincidence. Just sayin'.) Also, Cancerians tend to be visual people, so send nudes.

WHAT CANCERIANS CONSIDER CASUAL FIRST-DATE CONVERSATION

★ Where are you from?

★ What was the name of your first childhood pet?

★ What's your favorite line of your favorite episode of your favorite TV show?

★ Where were you when you first realized what you wanted to do with your life?

★ How do you see us spending the next 20 years together?

CANCER

How to blow their fucking minds

Cancerians don't fuck, they make love. And if you shuddered just reading that phrase, then this sign might not be for you. But get past the semantics and you may find yourself really enjoying Cancer's intensely passionate and sensual take on sex. Intimacy is a must, so let your Cancerian know how much you appreciate them. Slip into the shower with this water-loving sign and let things get steamy. And make sure you spend some time on Cancer's fave body part—the breasts. Men want them, women want attention lavished on them.

How to get what you need

Cancerians have a tendency to keep score, and that shit doesn't stop at the bedroom door. If you want something a little special in bed, your motto should be "Do unto others." A Cancerian will match your enthusiasm and generosity move for fucking move. Getting them to experiment might be a different story. This sign generally likes to stick with the classics, preferring comfort over adventure, but they can be persuaded to try new things if you put them at ease. The more loving and honest the relationship, the more creative the sex.

WITH CANCER FOR THE LONG HAUL

Deeply caring, kind, protective, and solid—this sign was built for relationships. But Cancerians expect a real partnership, someone who will be there for them through thick and thin. If they're not getting what they need, there's no fucking chance of you getting what you want. A Cancerian on the defensive will either lash out or withdraw completely. Avoid that by sharing the joys and the burdens equally with them and getting to know all of their (many) pet peeves. Also, learn to let go of the little shit, because God knows they won't.

How to have a great fucking partnership

Not gonna lie...you'll want to tell this sign to "pick a fucking mood and stick with it" more than a few times in your relationship. Your arguments aren't big blowups, they're never-ending tiffs—with Cancer bringing up the same shit time and time again. So, unless you want to be in an endless tug-of-war, you're going to have to suck it up sometimes. Just remind yourself that you'll never find anyone as thoughtful and considerate as a Cancerian. And definitely learn how to tell when their switch is about to flip.

How to deal with the day-to-day shit

Living with a Cancerian? Kiss any illusions you have about being in control of your household goodbye. The home is Cancer's domain, and they know just how they like it. Don't think for a second that means they'll be doing all the chores, though. As in all things, Cancerians expect to share responsibility equally. But they know both of you inside and out, so you'll be pleasantly surprised to find that your assigned tasks are things you don't really mind doing. And since the kitchen is also part of their domain, Cancerians tend to be damn good cooks.

How to ensure you'll be a cute-AF old couple

Cancerians are exactly the kind of people you want by your side through all the twists and turns of life. Those born under this sturdy, supportive sign will always be there to keep you grounded when you get overwhelmed. But there will be plenty of times you need to return the favor. Offer them comfort, security, and balance when they start to sweat the small stuff. And understand that, although they may retreat into themselves, they'll always come back out if you're patient. (Inside jokes can help pull them out—Cancerians love those.)

CANCER

IN THE CIRCLE OF TRUST WITH CANCER

CANCER IN YOUR SQUAD

Cancerians are those super-caring friends you can always count on. They're the ones who volunteer to be party mom, and the ones who still send actual cards on your birthday, and the ones go out of their way to make lunch happen despite being busy AF. They spend so much time worrying about other people that they can get hurt when friends don't return that effort. And they'll hold on to that shit without you even knowing it happened. So take a page from their (obviously detailed) book and practice a little empathy with your Cancerian friends.

How to have a fucking blast together

Sure, Cancerians can be a little picky when it comes to how they spend their downtime. But the main thing for them is just getting to spend time with one of their favorite people. Keep things cozy and low-key, like a cheese-and-wine night in or a pizza and beer lunch. (There should never not be food involved. That's, like, the first principle of Cancerian comfort.) Having learned from past mistakes, they'll only put forth as much effort as you do. So if they made the plans last time, it's your turn to step up.

How to get the tea

For a sign that's fucking steeped in feelings, it can be surprising difficult to get Cancerians to open up. But once they do, expect your cup to overflow. You can help get the ball rolling by talking to them in their own space, where they're most comfortable. Then spill some tea yourself, which makes them feel like they're one of the trusted few (even if you regularly announce that shit on your podcast). The most important thing is to let them know that you get where they're coming from. Feeling understood is everything for a Cancerian.

How to make things right

People born under this sign mate for life when it comes to friends, so they won't let a little squabble ruin your relationship. But they will hold on to it and tap into those hurt feelings whenever their mood swings low. Watch out for signs that you've crossed a line and try to walk things back immediately. If you hit a nerve, you'll get more than a little passive aggression. Just think of Cancer's crabby astrological counterpart—hard shell, soft insides, sharp fucking claws. Just make sure they know you would never intentionally upset them.

CANCER IN THE FAMILY

A Cancerian's affection for their home starts with a strong instinct to love, nurture, and protect their family. In an ideal situation, family provides the structure and stability that Cancerians crave. But since families are always crazy, it provides Cancerians the opportunity to impose some structure and stability by mothering everyone related to them (and many who aren't). This fiercely loyal sign wants what's best for their family members and will always be there to support them. Any coolness or distance is just a symptom of empathy overload.

How to have an awesome relationship with a Cancer parent

The nurturing force is strong with this one. Like, helicopter strong. These mother hens are affectionate, loving, and super protective. Thanks to their natural intuition, they know when something's not right with their kids, and they'll do anything to fix it. But in parenting as in all things, Cancerians need to learn to let the hell go. Forgive them for being a persnickety pain in the ass—they can't help it. And know that if they ever pull away, it has absolutely nothing to do with you. They just get lost in their own shit sometimes.

GOING ON GROUP VACAY WITH CANCER

Cancer [handing out binders]: Here are your tickets, hotel info, itinerary, and everyone's contact info. Don't lose this.

You: Do you think we can stop off at—

Cancer: No.

You: Ugh…I have a middle seat. Anyone want to trade?

Cancer [taking your binder]: I'll Venmo your refund.

CANCER

How to raise a kick-ass Cancer kid

Most kids have trouble expressing how they're feeling, but Cancerians are a special case. They're not just dealing with their own shit; they're also feeling the feelings of everyone around them. So they're going to need some help sorting things out. Make sure you give them the comfort and security they need, but encourage independent activities, too. Cancerian kids can get a bit clingy if you don't kick their asses out of the nest. Luckily, these little empaths have great imaginations and no problem channeling their energy into something productive.

How to go from siblings to BFFs

Growing up with siblings can be tricky for super-sensitive Cancerians. They're not the rough-and-tumble type, so they're likely to hold a grudge if they spent their childhood getting beat up by older brothers. And they're too earnest to deal with being mean-girled by sisters. These sweet souls do best with siblings who become friends. Once they do, Cancerians can let go of old grudges and focus on lavishing their loved ones with care and affection. (And if you're one of several siblings, get on their good side early. They totally play favorites.)

THE LAST WORD

Navigating Cancer's ever-shifting moods isn't always easy. But with this insider info, you're a hell of a lot more likely to see the sweet, pillowy soft insides of this hard-shelled sign. Basically, just have your shit together. And if you could also smack down chaos and drama like you're spiking a volleyball, the Cancerians in your life would really fucking appreciate it.

Cancer Motto

LET ME CHECK MY SCHEDULE

LEO

Fucking Awesome
(and They Know It)

AKA
The Lion

BIRTHDAY
July 23–August 22

SIGNS
Fire | Fixed | Masculine

RULED BY
The Sun

ON A GOOD DAY
Protective, Ambitious,
Generous

ON A BAD DAY
Narcissistic, Demanding,
Arrogant

FAMOUSLY LEO
Madonna,
Jennifer Lawrence,
Barack Obama

Being around Leo is like looking into the sun. This sign is full of bright, fiery, passionate, and dazzling people who, coincidentally, think the world revolves around them. You can't really fault them—with so many incredible attributes, they come by their narcissistic tendencies honestly. After all, Leos are creative, fearless, warm, loyal, and charming. Among this sign you'll find talented actors, super-successful CEOs, and badass neurosurgeons (the God complex is a dead giveaway). Leos fight for what they want, and they fucking get it. But it helps if they have someone like you to make sure they don't trip over their damn ego.

LEO

THAT 9-TO-5 GRIND WITH LEO

WORKING UNDER LEO

Like the lion they're named for, Leos charge straight into any challenge and just fucking demolish it. So it makes a lot of sense that you often find this sign at the top of the company food chain. And that's just where they like to be. Leo bosses walk around with a mental soundtrack of their employees chanting, "All hail the conquering hero." They demand respect and recognition for their accomplishments. But it's that ego, which alternately inspires and nauseates their staff, that sometimes keeps them from achieving greatness. If they can keep it in check, Leos make magnanimous leaders.

How to bring them your brilliant ideas

As long as you don't challenge their standing, Leos are all ears for good ideas. But these bosses see themselves as representatives of their teams, often taking the heat when their employees fuck up. So, to them, it only makes sense that they also claim the credit when their employees do well. In other words, don't be surprised if they pitch your awesome idea as their own. It's just the price you pay for having someone stand in front of you when the hyenas come. But Leo bosses will also fight for you if they believe in you, so good work is never wasted.

How to show them your A game

Leos appreciate great work when they see it. But these office heroes always want to be the brightest star, so don't ever try to outshine them. They'll consider it a challenge to their authority, which ends with them putting you in your place. Instead, welcome Leo into your wins. (This has the bonus of keeping your achievements fresh in their minds to bump any slip-ups farther down the list.) In a presentation scenario, break out all the stops. You need both style and function for a sign that likes the finer things in life.

How to keep it real

You know how certain work environments force you to get good at playing politics? Offices run by Leos fall into that category, so you're going to have to stroke their fragile ego if you want to get anything done. Thankfully, it's not that hard to low-key manipulate Leo into giving you what you need. The most important thing is to avoid even the appearance of questioning their authority. Instead, offer your suggestion and walk away, letting it simmer. Before long, Leo will think it was their idea in the first place.

LEO IN THE TRENCHES WITH YOU

Because Leo is always looking to move up, they're not really what you would call a "team player." This sign usually ends up competing more than collaborating, and that can leave their coworkers feeling like they have the imprint of an expensive loafer on their backs. But their competitive drive isn't vindictive. Leos love people (especially people who love them). They're truly just competing against themselves and don't realize that they may leave their coworkers feeling a little less than loving toward them.

How to get great shit done together

So how do you accomplish shit with someone who's in it to win it? You lean into that ambition. Leos are usually kick-ass workers who will shoulder more than their fair share of responsibility if there's a chance they'll be recognized for it. They'll also gladly do any task that's handed down from higher up. So give them their marching orders and get out of their way. And if that doesn't work, remember this: they fucking love a challenge that only they can tackle. It's all in how you word it.

ASKING YOUR LEO COWORKER FOR HELP

What you say: Hey, can you upload this file for me?

What Leo hears: I need you. You're the only one who can help. You're amazing. I love you.

How to become work besties

You might have your work cut out for you if you're trying to befriend one of the more motivated Leos. But there are still plenty of people born under this sign who want to have a good time with their coworkers. Hedge your bets by showing them that A) you can help them achieve their goals, or B) that you're happy to let them have the spotlight all to themselves. You could also just offer to buy them a fucking margarita on Taco Tuesday. That one really separates the fun Leos from the killjoys.

How to send out an SOS

Generous Leos are happy to help out a coworker in need. Sure, they might also think they're the only ones who can. But if they're fixing your fucking computer, don't look a gift lion in the teeth, you know? Just don't take up too much of their valuable time—they've got important shit to do. And they won't put their work on the back burner if it means losing even the tiniest bit of edge. In fact, you're probably better off just hitting up the nearest Taurean.

THE LEO EMPLOYEE

It'd be pretty hard for Leo to become the boss if they didn't spend any time eating sad cubicle salads. It'd be even harder if they sucked at their job, which is why the spend every working second kicking ass and taking names. Leos are loyal, invested, steadfast, and enthusiastic employees who will happily spend a lifetime working for the same company if there are enough rungs to climb on its ladder. This sign is not about that gig economy, so they're pretty fucking motivated to help a company succeed.

How to get them motivated

Leo's motivation is pretty simple: if they want to call themselves the best, they need to be the best. So people born under this sign are usually on top of their shit with or without oversight. But you can always tap into their need to be recognized for their expertise. Leo wants to be your right-hand guy. Help them get there by giving them clear instructions. (Like, crystal clear. Down-to-the-last-detail clear.) Without clarity, Leo can get a little carried away or, alternatively, totally stuck in their own indecision.

How to light a fire under their ass

Do you even have to ask? Dangling success and all of its trappings in front of Leo will have them busting through the cubicle wall like the fucking Kool-Aid man, trying to get you what you need. Financial reward and the clout of a promotion are both super-effective carrots. And if you don't have either of those handy, try raising their competitive hackles. The words, "You're the only one who can" have a way of winding Leo up. But at the end of the day, this sign's desire to do great work will probably be enough.

How to have the hard convos

Leos are usually so busy looking on the bright side that they can feel totally blindsided by bad news. Starting things off with a few hints can help soften the blow. And whatever you do, don't let things get too personal. Leos have pretty much three reactions to criticism: 1) feeling attacked and getting aggressive, 2) pouting like a kid who dropped their waffle cone, and 3) rising to a new challenge. You want Door #3. You don't have to sugarcoat the problem; you just have to give them the opportunity to fix it.

LOVE, SEX, AND FOR-EV-ER WITH LEO

THE LEO MEET-CUTE

You can usually find Leo at the center of a crowded room, performing surprisingly good karaoke or maneuvering a selfie stick for the most flattering shot. And even if you think that's obnoxious, you'll find yourself oddly drawn to them. This sign has magnetism on lock. Sure, Leos can be a bit much, but they're also kind, loyal, and generous partners. Despite the extroversion, Leo might be a little reserved with you at first. They're sizing you up, looking for signs that you have your shit together and harbor a healthy dose of ambition.

How to woo the shit out of them

This is an interview—act accordingly. A good first impression is crucial to Leo, who wants to be swept off their feet by someone who dresses well, speaks intelligently, and makes big moves in life. Romantic comedy gestures are more than welcome. Actual comedy…not so much. Leos can't really laugh at themselves, so skip the witty remarks. And while they hate false flattery, sincere flattery is a fucking requirement. But more than anything, they want to see that you're warm, caring, and passionate, like they are.

How to dazzle on your date

Dating Leo can be a bit of a tightrope act. Leos believe that their date's appearance and accomplishments reflect on them, and they want to be able to show you off proudly. But they'll worry about you dimming their own light by comparison. In other words, you have to shine brightly enough to be worthy of them, but you can't *outshine* them. They need to impress you. So let them pick the place. It's probably easier than trying to come up with one that's the right combination of public, engaging, and fun.

LEO

64

How to cut through the bullshit

You might be tempted to think that Leo's showboating is just bluster—that underneath it all is insecurity. Nope. This is just them. They want all the attention, and they feel they've earned it. (To be fair, they're usually pretty fucking accomplished. But even those who aren't can feel entitled to applause.) This sign has the kind of unbreakable confidence we all wish we had, so you might just choose to admire it. At least you'll always know where you stand with them because they're secure enough to admit how they feel.

BETWEEN THE SHEETS WITH LEO

When it comes to sex, Leos are here. for. it. Whenever, wherever, in whichever position. They're just very happy to be here. You could say it's refreshing to be with someone who has zero hang-ups. They're all good with their body image, they're not worried about getting caught in a risky place, and they have no issues asking for what they want. That doesn't mean they aren't constantly trying to improve their game—this is Leo, after all. So you're pretty much guaranteed to have a good time.

How to whet their appetite

For Leo, the foreplay starts long before you hit the bedroom (or the bathroom at the bar). They get turned on showing you off, so make sure you're serving looks and let them. Speaking of stroking their…egos, compliments are Leo's biggest aphrodisiac. You don't even have to go the obvious route of complimenting their appearance or sexual prowess. Any sort of praise will do the trick. And if you really want to rev their engine, start shit in public. Leo's love of attention translates into a bit of an exhibitionist streak.

SLIDING INTO A LEO'S DMS

@You: Hey, I loved that picture of you in the mountains

@Leo: I loved that picture of me too, lol!

LEO

How to blow their fucking minds

Leos have a secret: although they seem superficial, they're actually hopeless romantics at heart. Their best sex will always be with someone they love. If you're not there yet, making their fucking toes curl isn't a bad way to win their heart. But you're going to have to set your own ego aside to do that. (And maybe a little bit of your self-respect, too.) Ready for this? Leos want to be worshipped and adored like the gods and goddesses they know they are. Luckily, they don't expect you to reinvent the *Kama Sutra*. Enthusiasm is usually enough.

How to get what you need

Unsurprisingly, Leos can be a little preoccupied with their own orgasm. But you don't have to worry about getting yours, because these passionate paramours are always down for Round 2. And Round 3. (You may want to carb load and keep an ice pack handy.) And this is where their ego proves useful: even if Leo's initial instinct is to please themselves, they want to be the best you've ever had. That means they have to consider your needs. So, don't think twice about asking for what you want—you can fucking bet they will give it to you.

WITH LEO FOR THE LONG HAUL

A relationship with Leo is a "lasso the moon" kind of romance. Once you crack the surface on this sign, you'll find a loving, sincere, and bighearted partner who wants to give you the world. They will never stop trying to impress you and win you over, even if you're already hopelessly in love with them. Plus, these charming extroverts will fit right in with your family and friends, which is fucking awesome. (Ever have to defend a relationship to your parents? It's exhausting, so this is no small thing.) Leo might be a little high maintenance, but their love is absolutely worth maintaining.

How to have a great fucking partnership

If you're going to love a Leo, you can't be a whiny bitch about their ambition. This sign is always going to shoot for the fucking moon. If you ask them to choose between you and their career, you might not like the outcome. But if you can deal with their big dreams, you're in for a world-class romance. This sign loves a big gesture, and they have a way of helping you live in the moment. All they ask is that you appreciate and support them (even when they're being a narcissistic ass).

How to deal with the day-to-day shit

Leos want what they want, and they usually get it, so life will be easier for you if you let them take the lead. Pick your battles carefully, and make sure you stop to take a breath when things get heated—this fire sign can fight. But when something's really important to you, Leos are happy to calmly talk it out. (If you can get them to stop moving for a fucking minute, that is.) And since they're all about those creature comforts, they make a pretty damn cozy home. Just keep an eye on the budget.

How to ensure you'll be a cute-AF old couple

A relationship with Leo is #goals. All this dreamy sign wants to do is create an amazing life they can share with someone. So, when they meet that person, they go all in. Mirror their generosity, affection, passion, and idealism, and the two of you will spend your lives making each other happy. But you'll need to assure Leo of your love and devotion often. Their greatest fear—the thing that keeps them up at night—is that the love of their life might not truly love them back.

LEO

IN THE CIRCLE OF TRUST WITH LEO

LEO IN YOUR SQUAD

People are everything to Leo, whose contacts list includes pretty much everyone they've ever met. This sign collects friends from grade school to grad school and beyond. (Because, let's face it, more people equals more attention.) And although they don't have the same relationship with all of them, they're always happy to pick up wherever they left off. Leo is a true, thick-and-thin kind of friend— they're always there for you. But leaning on a Leo can get addictive, so make sure you remember how to stand on your own two feet when you need to.

How to have a fucking blast together

Don't expect Leo to sit still for a night in on the couch—they have a deep, clawing need to get the hell out of the house. These genuine extroverts feed off the energy of others, so think big. Grab a group of friends and head out for a day of paintball or laser tag, something that lets Leo prove they've got skills. Or just head out to a bar—there's always a pool table or a piano they can commandeer. Just give Leo plenty of advance notice so they can pencil you into their crazy-ass schedule.

How to get the tea

Leos love to gossip with friends (or, really, anyone within fucking earshot). But don't expect them to do it over WhatsApp. For this sign, everything is more fun in person and gossip is just another good reason to hang. That doesn't mean you should save the good shit for when you get together. Who knows when Leo will have a break in their schedule? And they'd rather get a text than be left out of the loop. Getting the scoop before anyone else is just another way for them to come out on top.

How to make things right

Did you tell Leo they weren't the best at something? Or, even worse, did you *beat them* at something? First of all, how dare you. Secondly, they're probably not even worried about it. They know they're the best, and they'll get your ass next time. But if you take advantage of their trust or take them for granted, you're going to have some ground to make up. Leo needs to know that you value their friendship. Tell them how much you need them in your life and all the ways they make it better—details matter.

LEO IN THE FAMILY

This is a sign that sees attention as love. They need to both give it and get it from those closest to them to feel whole. (It's kind of like middle-child syndrome, except they could be the only child and still act up.) But they also believe that having the spotlight means they can shine it on those around them. So Leos radiate this joy—they just throw that shit around like confetti. Although they're bound to bring some fucking drama to your family, it's a small price to pay for the joy they bring with it.

How to have an awesome relationship with a Leo parent

This sign can be kind of a conundrum when it comes to parenting. On one hand, Leo's chill, live-in-the-moment vibe can disappear when they have kids—they foist all their ambitions onto them. On the other, Leo can be an absentee parent because they're so focused on their own shit. But right in the middle is a super-affectionate Leo parent who loves to explore and have fun, reveling in the adoration of their little ones. If you get that middle ground even every so often, count yourself very lucky. The rest of the time, just know how much you're loved.

**TOP 5 REASONS
LEO > A LIFE COACH**

1. Acts like your personal affirmation-a-day calendar

2. Can style looks to help you fuck with your ex

3. Models self-confidence like a fucking boss

4. Will get your self-pitying ass off the couch and into the bar

5. Is always down for some retail therapy

LEO

How to raise a kick-ass Leo kid

Leo is Leo, right from the start. These kids are confident and bold, born to be fucking stars. Their leadership abilities make them an asset in school, where they pull student-of-the-month on the regular. And they have more friends than you can count. Give this high-energy sign plenty of freedom to explore and express themselves. But also give them the structure they need to learn how to use their gifts for good (and not for narcissistic garbage). Encourage their best traits—generosity, kindness, and positivity—so they don't lean on their more self-indulgent tendencies and you'll have one amazing fucking human on your hands.

How to go from siblings to BFFs

How much a Leo needs the spotlight can depend a lot on their siblings. If they spent their younger years competing against you and losing, you can expect them to be more of a pain in the ass later on (so, thanks for that). But if they were top dog, you probably saw Leo's more loving and protective side. Either way, you can start fresh as adults. Go on extroverted adventures together, and let Leo feel needed. And for the love of everything holy, let them brag about how awesome they are once in a while.

THE LAST WORD

All set to share in the warm glow of Leo's personal spotlight? Just remember the gist of life with Leo: helping them expand that spotlight is the best way to be a part of it. When you embrace this sign's ambition (and avoid bruising their fragile fucking ego), you get all the perks of their passion, fearlessness, charm, and lion-like loyalty.

Leo Motto

I GOT THIS

VIRGO
Perfectly Imperfect

AKA
The Maiden

BIRTHDAY
August 23–September 22

SIGNS
Earth | Mutable | Feminine

RULED BY
Mercury

ON A GOOD DAY
Organized, Rational, Resourceful

ON A BAD DAY
Perfectionist, Obsessive, Anxious

FAMOUSLY VIRGO
Freddy Mercury, Beyoncé, Adam Sandler

Virgos have a reputation for being crazy-critical perfectionists, but this sign is so much more than their more nitpicky tics. Sure, they're detail people. And they know how to achieve a damn goal—this sign can get it. But everything they do is to improve the lives of others. If their inner critic is bugging you, take solace in knowing that it's bugging them, too. They're twice as hard on themselves as they are on anyone else. So they need people like you to remind them that progress *is* perfection and that even their flaws are beautiful.

THAT 9-TO-5 GRIND WITH VIRGO

WORKING UNDER VIRGO

Cards on the table: working under Virgo can be rough. This sign has some sky-high standards, unrealistic expectations, and intense methods. But if you can handle the heat, they'll help forge you into a better version of yourself. Virgo bosses are constantly pushing their employees. As realists, they know when something's unachievable. They just think you should strive anyway. People born under this sign can't stomach mediocrity, and they're definitely not here for any lazy, entitled bullshit. When you work for Virgo, you achieve greatness or die trying. (Or quit and find a Libra to work for.)

How to bring them your brilliant ideas

Remember when you had to present research papers in science class? Channel that energy into whatever you bring to your Virgo boss. They need that shit in writing, with all the facts laid out in detail and a summary at the top. Don't bother editorializing when you present it, either. Let the information stand on its own and Virgo will draw their own conclusions. Just be prepared to slash the budget; this sign is all about doing more with less. And make sure you know your shit—there *will* be a quiz.

How to show them your A game

Virgo bosses care about one thing—results—and they know who's getting them. This boss sees all, so make sure they're seeing your dedication, decisiveness, and economy. If they catch you sending cat videos to your work bestie over Slack, you're fucked. (Just kidding—they would never use a fun, camaraderie-enabling service like Slack.) Time is money, and they don't want to see you wasting either one. The best way to stay on a Virgo boss's good side is to keep your head down and do the work. Also, they love a little value added.

How to keep it real

Managing a Virgo manager takes some doing. From the unrealistic demands to the unnecessary finger pointing, Virgo bosses are basically every cartoon boss ever. (Except Mr. Burns, who is definitely a Capricorn.) If you fucked up, own it and immediately tell them how you plan to fix it. There's no other way out. If you didn't fuck up, bring the facts and leave your indignation at the door. Virgo responds to logic, not emotion. And when you need your boss to agree to something, tell them why it's a win for the company—an economical one.

VIRGO IN THE TRENCHES WITH YOU

Mercifully, Virgo coworkers have way more chill than their managerial brethren. They respect the hell out of their team, and they actually enjoy making friends at work. Plus, their perfectionism means they're physically incapable of shirking responsibilities or letting you down. These quiet cubicle dwellers are happiest to let others stand in the spotlight while they go about their business, kicking ass and taking names. Politely. (You'll never find super-considerate Virgo microwaving salmon in the breakroom.) Don't be tempted to take advantage of their goodwill, though, or you'll get their wrath instead.

How to get great shit done together

Virgo's generosity and badass abilities in organization and research make teaming up with this sign a no-brainer. But because they're used to working independently, they may need a minute to adjust. Giving your Virgo coworker control of the project can help them feel comfortable more quickly. You could also let them handle the spreadsheets and data points while you work on the creative side of things. Just make sure you do your part. Virgos will bend over backward to help someone, but they're not going to put up with any freeloading bullshit.

INTERVIEWING A VIRGO

You [flipping through 30 pages of résumé]: Do you have any experience with spreadsheets?

Virgo: Yes. See page 6, section B, subsection iii.

VIRGO

How to become work besties

Combine Virgo's reputation for being a workaholic perfectionist with their tendency to keep a low profile, and you might not realize just how great these folks are. The kind, caring folks born under this sign genuinely like people. They want to grab drinks at lunch and bitch about the marketing department by the water cooler. You just have to give them the chance. Letting them vent to you about work is one of the best ways to get to know them. Just be prepared to explain your jokes—this sign doesn't really get sarcasm.

How to send out an SOS

Need help with your schedule? Organizing your office? Project research? Call a Virgo. But definitely don't ask them to weigh in on your love life. Virgos relate to people like people relate to their pets—they love them, but they don't always understand why they do what they do. But Virgo totally understands why that value is showing up on your spreadsheet, and they're thrilled to help you understand it, too. You might just have to ask them to slow down when explaining shit—their brain sometimes works faster than their mouth.

THE VIRGO EMPLOYEE

Virgo's perfectionist tendencies might be nightmarish in a boss, but they're a fucking godsend in an employee. This super-reliable sign gets shit done and done well, especially if it has anything to do with problem solving, research, and organization. Virgos are also awesome at fixing broken systems and developing even better ones. And they're just as happy to work with others as they are to go it alone. Give them some proper instructions (numbered lists and bullet points preferred) and watch 'em go!

How to get them motivated

As great as Virgos are at detail work, they don't want to sit there and address fucking envelopes for hours. (They also don't want to work with the boss's son-in-law who doesn't know what the fuck he's doing and doesn't care. This sign has no patience for idiots or assholes.) These smarties want to put their gifts to good use. Give them a real challenge and watch their brain rev up to meet it. Whether it's a puzzle to solve or a multi-tiered project to organize, they'll just be thrilled to put their thinking cap on.

How to light a fire under their ass

Virgo's meticulous methods can sometimes get in the way of them getting shit done quickly. But because they love a challenge, just giving them a deadline should be incentive to speed things up. If they're dragging their feet for other reasons, you can try dangling a carrot: praise or promotion—your choice. But remember that these are positive-reinforcement people. If you're angry, you better do some fucking breathing exercises before you talk to them. Come at them hard and they'll just power down (or melt down).

How to have the hard convos

Like most of us (except Leo), Virgos can suffer from imposter syndrome, and that can send them to a dark place when they get called out. So go easy when you have to sit them down. Remember that those in this sensitive sign are incredibly hard on themselves. The last thing you want to see is a Virgo spinning out—they hold a lot of shit in, and things will get ugly if it all comes pouring out at once. A little constructive criticism will go a long way toward getting you what you want without breaking your best employee.

VIRGO

LOVE, SEX, AND FOR-EV-ER WITH VIRGO

THE VIRGO MEET-CUTE

Virgos have a harder time than most putting themselves out there, which means relinquishing a little more control than they'd like. (Shocker.) Because they tend to trust algorithms more than people, you're more likely to meet up with Virgo by swiping right. They can be a little cool at first, but their silence isn't judgment. (Well, it isn't *always* judgment.) Virgos can just get lost in the recesses of their own minds. This sign believes in quality over quantity, so once they find a connection with someone, they're likely to stick around.

How to woo the shit out of them

When you first start talking to Virgo, keep things very chill. Maybe get to know each other over text for a while before meeting up. (They're going to want to rewrite each text like twelve times, and they can't do that in person.) When you do meet, go somewhere quiet and relaxed, like a coffee shop. This sign wants to know that you can hold your own in a conversation. They like a little wit (as long as they can understand it) and a little sparkle, but they love insightful commentary. And they're wary of flash— Virgos need to know if they like the *real* you.

How to dazzle on your date

Once you've passed Virgo's initial testing phase, you can finally go on a real-life date! Make sure you pick a place *they* like rather than showing off a favorite of yours. Virgo's disappointment is not subtle, and there's no point in letting them ruin the shit you love. Somewhere in all of that preamble, they probably mentioned a few safe options. If not, definitely ask. Impressing Virgo is just a matter of having your shit together and putting a little thought into things. This sign loves a planner (because they *cannot* roll with the punches).

How to cut through the bullshit

First and foremost, take any complaining with a margarita-rim of salt. Virgos are born perfectionists, and they can be a little much when things aren't just so. It really is them, not you, and they know it. You can try to read their mood, but at some point, you just gotta go for it. Order the dessert-for-two, lean in for the kiss, ask for the second date—whatever. Just do what you can to get past Virgo's prickly exterior so you can get to know the kindhearted person inside.

BETWEEN THE SHEETS WITH VIRGO

Although this sign is represented by the Maiden, Virgos are anything but virginal. They view sex as a basic need, like food and water. That doesn't mean their sex life is basic, though. Just like a delicious meal, they like their sex life spicy. This is the one area where Virgos can completely let loose and release all of their (many) frustrations. It's like having an alter ego that only select people get to see. But don't expect to see Superman while Clark Kent's working—there's a time and a place for that shit.

How to whet their appetite

With Virgo, you need to do more than warm them up. You need to melt away their insecurities. Make sure the time and place are right for some relaxation, then let this sign know how sexy they are. Bonus points if your appreciation ventures beyond Virgo's appearance. But don't worry too much about being super smooth and seductive—this sign likes a little inexperience. Plus, turning you on turns them on. And they're really fucking good at it because, as talented researchers, they've taken the time to study your likes and dislikes.

GETTING TO KNOW VIRGO

What Virgo says: Tell me about yourself.

What Virgo means: Tell me about your childhood, your biggest fears, your relationship with your mom, your favorite flavor of ice cream, and who you voted for in the last election.

How to blow their fucking minds

This is the one area of their life where Virgos feel comfortable enough to explore and experiment, so you better make it worth their fucking while. Be open to whatever they want to try or let them teach you something new. Make them feel wanted. Show Virgo that you're willing to put in some effort to learn what they like and give them what they want. And don't be afraid of a little role-play. This dominant sign is finally ready to surrender control—they want you to take it.

How to get what you need

You don't have to say or do a damn thing to get what you want when you're sleeping with a Virgo. This sign is constantly clocking you. They study your reactions and adjust accordingly, always trying to improve their performance. These perfectionists need to please you in order to enjoy themselves. So let them. But if you want to help them out by giving them a hint here and there, they won't mind. This is the one area of their life where they're happy to take orders.

WITH VIRGO FOR THE LONG HAUL

Virgos are built to create stable, loving relationships. Sure, their perfectionism can be a pain in the ass, but it can also be a real asset. They're on top of anything that requires planning. And because they do their fucking research, you know that anything they plan will go smoothly. They also apply that inexhaustible work ethic to making their partnership work and making their loved ones happy. Virgo will always support you and help you grow into the person you want to be. In return, they just need a little patience for their more persnickety moments.

How to have a great fucking partnership

This sign is used to barreling forward at full speed, so they need a partner who can help them find balance before they have a breakdown. Getting them to laugh is a start. Lightening their load should be the ultimate goal. Virgo doesn't make it easy for others to share the burden, but they can get used to the idea if you ease them into it. You, however, will have to get used to being wrong. (In Virgo's mind, if you're not doing it the way they would do it, you're doing it wrong.) But they'll eventually learn that done is better than perfect.

How to deal with the day-to-day shit

You should know by now to leave the planning to your Virgo partner. Going along with what they want will make your life easier, and they're just better at it anyway. Are you going to spend a fucking hour researching the best price for your flight? Probably not. So let them—they live for it. As for the rest of it, they like to divvy things up evenly. Do your part and they'll do theirs. But do it their way or you'll fucking hear about it, which is like being slowly pecked to death by a small bird.

How to ensure you'll be a cute-AF old couple

Virgo needs someone chill to balance out all of that anxious energy, but they also need someone who's mentally stimulating. And the chemistry has to be fire. They're not about to spend eternity having vanilla sex. (Sorry, Taurus.) Ironically, you'll need to help them expand their comfort zone in every other respect. The most important thing to this sign is your happiness, so if you need something, speak up. Virgo is a mutable sign, which means they can change their ways, especially if it's necessary to make a relationship work.

VIRGO

IN THE CIRCLE OF TRUST WITH VIRGO

VIRGO IN YOUR SQUAD

These steadfast besties are always there when you need them and they are happy to be needed. But because Virgo is used to having a handle on their own shit, they hate to ask for help themselves. (You know they're fucking desperate if they're asking someone else what to do.) Hit Virgo up when you need a logical perspective or someone to plan your engagement party. And just nod and smile if they ever delve into matters of the heart. This super-rational sign tends to miss social cues and can give out some really crappy advice.

How to have a fucking blast together

Virgos don't need to be in constant contact, but they do love to catch up with friends. Keep things one-on-one for these busy introverts. (Unless you're on the hunt. Virgo makes one hell of a wingman/woman.) Letting this sign plan the when/where/what of it all will save you the headache of being micromanaged over a fucking brunch date. In fact, let them plan your major life celebrations, too. You'll get to enjoy time together while Virgo does what they do best. (Just don't expect them to attend—not enough champagne in the world for that much social interaction.)

How to get the tea

Once you befriend Virgo and break through their cool exterior, you won't have to try very hard to get them to open up. (You may have to learn how to interpret their subtweets, though.) Get Virgo to open up by finding common ground—they love a good bitch session back-and-forth. And despite their "above the fray" attitude, they can't help themselves when it comes to good gossip. But be warned: Virgos are judgy. They just are. So if you don't feel like fucking hearing about it, keep your shit to yourself.

How to make things right

To be honest, it's so easy to offend Virgo that it's almost not worth worrying about. Their perfectionism turns even the tiniest, unintended slight into a whole thing. You will fuck up. You can't help it. (Unless you're some sort of AI that they, themselves, programmed. Even then, it's probably still fucking possible.) The little stuff, they can forgive. But if you change the game on them, you have to do the legwork to earn back their trust. Holding up your end of any bargain is crucial when you're friends with this sign.

VIRGO IN THE FAMILY

Virgos will always put the happiness of others before their own, but never is this truer than with their family. This sign will bend over backward to be whatever their parent, child, or sibling needs, taking on the role of protector, supporter, disciplinarian, and peacekeeper. They can wear themselves out with all of that effort, so make sure you remind them to fill their own cup once in a while. And don't let their trademark criticism get under your skin—it really does come from a place of love.

How to have an awesome relationship with a Virgo parent

Anxious people make anxious parents, and Virgo is no exception. This sign's protective instincts can go into hyperdrive when they have kids. That rigid need for obedience often results in the exact opposite of obedience, which basically drives everyone in the house batshit. But in their heart of hearts, Virgo wants their kids to see them as a friend. If you can, keep your rebellion on the DL. And show up for every holiday and reunion with a smile on your face—traditions are no joke to this sign. They will nitpick. Just learn to let it roll off your fucking back.

"PRAISE" FROM A VIRGO MOM

"I love everything you've done with your new house. It's just so… cozy…and you do so much with so little. I'm so proud of you for striking out on your own. So what if you end up alone and childless? This house is perfect for just you."

VIRGO

How to raise a kick-ass Virgo kid

Virgo's obsessive tendencies start early, and these sweet kids will work their asses off to be perfect for you. Virgo children can hold a crazy family together all by themselves. So make sure that burden never falls on them, and that you show them some appreciation for their efforts. Teach these kids kindness and forgiveness while you're at it—the fucking judginess also starts early. And definitely get them a dog or some other furry creature to love. The unconditional love will make them more compassionate, resilient, and affectionate humans.

How to go from siblings to BFFs

This loyal and loving sign will always have a sibling's back. Virgos want a strong, cohesive family unit, so they have zero desire to compete with siblings. But they will absolutely throw down if shit isn't fair or if parents play favorites. Make sure that there's a give-and-take between siblings, and address any injustices (real or perceived) head-on. Once you're on a good footing, your Virgo sibling will spend their life challenging you and helping you become the best version of yourself. Try returning the favor by gently nudging them out of their own comfort zone.

THE LAST WORD

Next time Virgo's perfectionism is pissing you off, remember that they really can't help it. (It comes from a good, if occasionally misguided, place.) A little patience and hard data can go a long way in smoothing over any Virgo-related issues. But when all else fails, make them laugh. God knows Virgos need a little levity in their overly structured lives!

Virgo Motto

DO AS I SAY...AND AS I DO

LIBRA
Fucking Switzerland

AKA
The Scales

BIRTHDAY
September 23–October 22

SIGNS
Air | Cardinal | Masculine

RULED BY
Venus

ON A GOOD DAY
Diplomatic, Peaceful,
Charming

ON A BAD DAY
Passive-Aggressive,
Indecisive, Self-Absorbed

FAMOUSLY LIBRA
Oscar Wilde,
Brie Larson, Donald Glover

Blessed are the Libras—er, peacemakers. Same thing. The beautiful, caring souls born under this sign can't stand conflict. And with their natural charm and top-notch communication skills, they have no problem helping people avoid it. Libra's deep sense of empathy and desire for fairness help them see both sides of any argument (a blessing and a curse). But their need to please people and keep the peace can also turn this softhearted sign into a doormat. When it's all too much, Libras retreat into themselves. Prove deserving of Libra's affection and you'll never have a better boss, lover, or friend.

LIBRA

THAT 9-TO-5 GRIND WITH LIBRA

WORKING UNDER LIBRA

Libras are some of the best fucking humans on Earth, so it only makes sense that working for one would be rewarding. They offer a collaborative environment and they consider team spirit an important tenet of their business. Libra encourages their employees to help each other up in a world that often sees people stepping over each other instead. Between their kindness and their inclusive, open-door approach to work, this sign inspires some of their employees' best work. People want to do them proud. This sign isn't without its faults, but you'll love working for them anyway.

How to bring them your brilliant ideas

First and foremost, let Libra know you have their back. This sign is people-focused, so these bosses will always be more concerned with how an idea affects their team than how it affects the company's bottom line. Libras also prioritize beauty and romance, so don't underestimate the power of pretty visuals. An attractive presentation will always be better received than a dull one. (Take a minute to make sure you're just as well put-together as your idea. Even a sloppily tucked shirt can lose you points with Libra.)

How to show them your A game

The good of others always comes first for Libra, so these leaders are impressed most by team players who look out for their coworkers. They don't want to see any ego or money grubbing in their department (so look out, Leos and Caps). Don't get it twisted, though—Libra will squish you like a bloodsucking bug if you take advantage of their selflessness. And never try to outshine them. Although Libras make magnanimous bosses, they're not going to tolerate ambitious employees eyeing up their gorgeous corner office. Stick to showing them that you can pull together with others and get shit done.

Libra's warm and fuzzy vibe isn't all rainbows and kittens—it can actually get them into trouble. This sign's need to be liked can get in the way of them getting shit done. And their desire to hear from everyone can cause a pileup of indecision. (They want to be fair to their employees, their boss, their clients, the intern in the mailroom, and the guy who delivers their sandwiches.) Help them get past this by presenting a clear winner. And maybe keep the small things off their desk so they don't hold stuff up.

LIBRA IN THE TRENCHES WITH YOU

Every team needs a Libra—someone to settle the arguments, deflate warring egos, and make everyone's day a little brighter. This sign is amazing at stepping back and seeing the big picture, allowing them to find the common ground your team can agree on. Aside from much-needed perspective, they also bring creativity and communication skills to the table. Be careful, though. These sweet talkers have no problem getting you on board with their crazy ideas. (They also love a good practical joke, so check your workstation carefully on April 1st.)

How to get great shit done together

Libras have a bad habit of pulling on loose threads that were better left alone, but it's only because they want to create better systems that benefit everyone. These out-of-the-box thinkers always have fresh ideas at the ready. They might not all be winners, but they'll definitely help you out of a rut. When this air sign gets carried away with their thoughts, they need you to reel them in. Point out flaws in their logic, and don't let them talk you into crazy shit. If you can harness their helpfulness, there's nothing you can't accomplish together.

TOP 3 REASONS LIBRA'S LATE TO WORK

1. They were cleaning their elderly neighbor's gutters

2. They had to frost the elaborate calculator cake they made for Sarah in Accounting's birthday

3. They couldn't decide which shoes to wear

LIBRA

How to become work besties

Becoming friends with Libra is easy—basically, you just can't be a selfish asshole. This sign loves people and sees the best in everyone. But if you want to be in Libra's tribe, you have to look on the bright side with them, look out for others, and put good shit into the world. They can't deal with the Debbie Downers who drain their high-vibe energy. Their best friends have a job to do, though. They need to protect Libra from their own need to be liked. Not everyone is worthy of this sign's goodwill.

How to send out an SOS

Libra is definitely one of the most generous, open-hearted signs. But like anyone, they can get a little wrapped up in their own shit sometimes. They might actually be so busy working on an idea to help the whole team that they're too damn distracted to help a single coworker with a specific problem. That doesn't mean they don't want to help. As long as you can get them to focus, they're an amazing resource. If you've got beef with another employee, Libra can help you broker a deal. They'll fight for fairness, even if it means dealing with a little conflict.

THE LIBRA EMPLOYEE

You know those job ads that inexplicably ask for a candidate to be both a team player and an independent worker? They're looking for a Libra. This sign is happy to work alone or with others, and they're effective as hell either way. Like other air signs, Libras are super smart, quick thinking, and full of great ideas. They're also natural-born helpers who just want to make everything better. No, they're not perfect. They do hold their company and coworkers to some fairly high standards. But as far as employees go, they're still pretty fucking great.

How to get them motivated

Libra's high standards are born of both a desire for fairness and the fact that they're smarter than the average bear (or lion, or crab). People who can't keep up bug them just as much as people who don't pull their own damn weight. If there's a lot of that going around in your office, you might want to assign tasks to Libra independently. They'll be much more motivated to get shit done when they're not distracted by people who aren't living up to their expectations.

How to light a fire under their ass

The naturally helpful folks born under this sign are happy to roll up their sleeves and crank shit out when they need to, but they have their limits. Libras are all about balance (their symbol is literally scales). They need to know that there's some respite at the end of a long road. Crack the whip too often, and this normally chill sign will rip it out of your fucking hands. When you need something asap, the solution is simple: take everything else off Libra's plate so they can focus.

How to have the hard convos

Libras know how awesome they are. They're not assholes about it, but they know. So it's really hard for them to hear that they're doing something wrong or that something's not working out. These silver-tongued sweethearts might even try to charm you into changing your mind. But if the bad news isn't a criticism of them, Libras are usually pretty good at going with the flow. Well, as long as that flow is fair to them, doesn't ask them to do more work than anyone else, and doesn't affect their upcoming vacay.

LIBRA

LOVE, SEX, AND FOR-EV-ER WITH LIBRA

THE LIBRA MEET-CUTE

See that beautiful, eloquent, charming human over there giving off Disney princess vibes? Probably a Libra. This sign seems to travel with their own sunshine and singing mice. With one conversation, they can make you feel lighter and more at ease. By the end of it, you'll probably think the date was your idea. But it was that Libra twinkle. Not only do those born under this sign understand people, communicate well, and make friends easily, but they also go after what they want. And if what they want is you, they'll sweep you off your fucking feet.

How to woo the shit out of them

Libras are looking for their own personal happily ever after, so they're not interested in any misunderstood villains or scrappy sidekicks. They want the hero who fights for justice and busts out the grand romantic gestures to win their hearts. This sign is in love with love, and they enjoy the hell out of a crush. Plus, Libras suffer from a superficial streak—appearances (and smells) matter. But more than anything, they just need to know that you're a good person who's trying to make the world better in some small way.

How to dazzle on your date

For such an idealistic sign, Libra are surprisingly easy to impress. The natural beauty of life and its delightful little moments are enough to make this sign smile. They crave simplicity, so you don't want to do anything too showy right out of the gate. Think: a starlit overlook or an intimate little bistro—one with some really fucking good food. Appealing to the senses is always a solid play. Witty conversation is a must—Libras love to laugh and exercise their minds at the same time. And if you're kind and thoughtful, you're already ahead of the game.

LIBRA

How to cut through the bullshit

Libras won't intentionally bullshit you, but these people pleasers tend to show you the best version of themselves. You'll have to ask good questions to get to know the person behind that ever-smiling mask of theirs. And although they have a reputation for superficiality, they're not about status, money, or accomplishment. They just have an oddly Shakespearean relationship with beauty—like, they just want to write sonnets about flower petals at sunset. But as far as their partner in life goes, they're just looking for someone who's smart, funny, and values balanced the way they are.

BETWEEN THE SHEETS WITH LIBRA

When it comes to sex, Libras can't just flip a switch—they need a little romance and seduction to get them in the mood. But this sign pulls out all the stops between the sheets. Just as unselfish and generous in bed as they are in life, Libras will always work hard to get shit right and please their partner. But you damn well better access your inner people pleaser and get to work, too. Remember, it's all about balance. (And savoring the moment. You're going to want to set aside some time for this sign.)

How to whet their appetite

You can't just pull a Naked Man move on Libra and expect to get laid. When you want to seduce this sign, old-school romance is the way. Making sure you look and smell good is your first priority. Then you can get things going with some PG fun: show up with a bouquet of flowers, savor a great dessert together, go for a walk in the moonlight on a summer night. Nothing turns Libra on more than enjoying the moment with someone special. (Except maybe fighting with them. These peacemakers love makeup sex.)

> **HOW LIBRA REACTS TO BEING ASKED OUT**
>
> [Waltzes around the living room, singing "So Close" from *Enchanted*, and forgets to reply.]

LIBRA

How to blow their fucking minds

Sex with this sign is a marathon, not a sprint. The stamina is real, so you better clear your schedule and limber up. Libras love to take things slow and savor the experience. They want to feel a sensual connection with their partner. And with all that time to fill, they're going to need a little more than missionary from you. This sign is all about adapting to their partner's needs, and they expect the same in return. So pay attention...and maybe pick up the latest issue of *Cosmo* for some creative ideas.

How to get what you need

Libras will literally bend over backward to make their partner happy, but that doesn't mean they're really comfortable doing it. They just have a hard time speaking up. So, by all means, ask for what you want. Libras have a library of skills and positions at the ready, and they're good with getting inventive. But pay close attention to their body language when they're trying something you like. If it seems like there's a disconnect, talk things out. Libras can always find a compromise that will satisfy everyone.

WITH LIBRA FOR THE LONG HAUL

Unsurprisingly, these hopeless romantics love being in relationships. Libras are all-in and ready to make your life look like a damn rom-com. Sure, they can be a little clingy. But they're a true partner—someone to celebrate all of your successes and support you during downturns. You can deal with some damn clinginess for that. What you'll want to put a stop to is Libra looking for you to complete them and changing who they are so that they complete you. But if you can find your balance together, you're in for one incredible relationship.

How to have a great fucking partnership

This is one of the best signs to have by your side in life. Not only do Libras help you live in the moment, but they're also great at defusing any tension. (Whether you're out with friends or fighting over the remote, that shit comes in handy.) And Libras go out of their way to make relationships work. That can be to their detriment, though. Because they're constantly deferring to you, it's like pulling fucking teeth to find out what they really want. But balance is the key to making your Libra happy, and they'll appreciate the effort.

How to deal with the day-to-day shit

When you live with a sign that's consumed by the concept of fairness, you can count on dividing the day-to-day shit evenly. Luckily for you, Libras also live to make their partner happy. So if you hate loading the fucking dishwasher, let them know. They can always come up with a better way to divvy shit up. But let them run the family's social calendar—you'll always be on time and you'll never be bored. And give them free rein over the aesthetics. Libras want a beautiful home, and they're a hell of a lot better at designing one than cleaning it.

How to ensure you'll be a cute-AF old couple

Keeping the romance alive is the best way to make old age with Libra still feeling like lovestruck teenagers. As long as you show this sign your love and appreciation, you'll get it back in fucking spades. But watch out for Libra's trademark alternative to confrontation: passive aggression. Because these partners hate conflict, they can let the little things fester until they become very big things. Make sure you talk shit out before it turns into a fight and Libra will make sure your life together is all wine and roses.

LIBRA

IN THE CIRCLE OF TRUST WITH LIBRA

LIBRA IN YOUR SQUAD

Libra friends are the fucking best. (Noticing a theme here?) When others go low, Libras go high. They always want the best for you. And thanks to their observational skills and deep understanding of human nature, Libras are basically built-in therapists. Who couldn't use one of those? The generous and thoughtful folks born under this sign are always up for a good time and helping you celebrate the beauty of everyday life. Plus, these social butterflies are experts in integrating new friends with old and making everyone feel comfortable and welcome.

How to have a fucking blast together

Libra can have fun while doing literally anything. Seriously—they can make standing in line at the fucking DMV fun. As long as they're hanging with their favorite people, they're enjoying the moment. Even if that moment involves unflattering government-issued ID photos. (J/k—Libra's physically incapable of taking an unflattering picture.) This sign loves to show people a good time. And because they know you so well, they know just how to make you smile. But if you make *them* decide where to hang, you may as well grab a beer while you wait.

How to get the tea

Think of Libra like Gemini but with more moral fiber. In other words, these expert communicators know the tea but aren't going to spill it if it means burning someone in the process. And getting them to open up about their own feelings when they're busy worrying about yours ain't easy. First, they need to know that you're OK. Then, they need to know they can trust you. But this sign really does love to share (they have a tag list a fucking mile long). So if you're in the inner circle, you'll be first to know what's going on.

How to make things right

If you've let down a Libra, it probably has something to do with upsetting the balance. First, find a way to stabilize things. Then apologize. This peace-loving sign wants to forgive you (they're allergic to grudges, and being mad at you is making them itch), but they need to see that you give a shit that you've upset them. Knowing that you feel bad is usually enough to smooth things over. But if you fuck with Libra too often, you're done. You can only walk on a doormat so many times before you wear it out.

LIBRA IN THE FAMILY

If Libra is that generous and loving with their coworkers and friends, just imagine how they are with family. These kindhearted people will do anything to make their loved ones happy. And that peacemaker shit can come in handy when your brother is brandishing a turkey leg at your uncle over a Thanksgiving dinner political argument. But Libra can get burnt out really quickly if they have to deal with a lot of family drama, so they may keep their distance at times. For the sake of their sanity, try to keep things chill.

How to have an awesome relationship with a Libra parent

In no parenting scenario ever will Libra be the "bad cop." All of the love, kindness, encouragement, and support that naturally occurs in Libra bubbles up and spills out onto their kids. They're the kind of parent who easily becomes a friend because they truly want to understand their children and let them be themselves. Everything they do is for their kids. As you get older, try to return the favor and get to know your Libra parent as well as they know you. (And thank them for all the ice cream they slipped you while you were grounded.)

ASKING LIBRA FOR THEIR OPINION

@You: What do u think? Dump him?
@Libra: [Graciously lists all the pros and cons without actually giving an opinion.]

@You: Ugh...so confused! Which candidate should I vote for?!
@Libra: [Graciously lists all the pros and cons without actually giving an opinion.]

@You: What do you think of these earrings with this dress?
@Libra: Oh honey, no. Be there in 5.

LIBRA

How to raise a kick-ass Libra kid

Libra kids are the bright lights of the family. Their generosity and love of fairness make them one hell of a playground buddy, so they'll always have friends. But these same qualities can make them an easy mark, so teach your little Libra boundaries. Let them know that disagreements are just a part of life and nothing to worry about. Thanks to their innate gifts, they'll always know intuitively how to handle a scuffle. And for the love of every dinner plan they'll ever make, please teach them how to make a fucking decision.

How to go from siblings to BFFs

Libras consider their siblings to be built-in besties. This sign will always have your back, especially if they think you're being treated unfairly. They'll also make you laugh when you want to cry. But kids will be kids, and there may have been times when you antagonized each other. Your Libra sibling probably swallowed their outrage whenever you acted like an asshole, making it a little too easy to walk all over them. Try to catch yourself when you fall back into old habits. And carve out some quiet quality time to spend with the sibling who adores you.

THE LAST WORD

Now that you know just how fucking awesome Libras are, you have to ask yourself: Am I worthy of the Libra in my life? Because this sign will have your back no matter what. Have theirs by encouraging some much-needed self-care. (And maybe also by kicking the ass of anyone who tries to take advantage of Libra's people-pleasing tendencies. Someone has to.)

Libra Motto

GOOD VIBES ONLY

SCORPIO

Not to Be
Fucked With

AKA
The Scorpion

BIRTHDAY
October 23–November 21

SIGNS
Water | Fixed | Feminine

RULED BY
Pluto

ON A GOOD DAY
Magnetic, Ambitious,
Imaginative

ON A BAD DAY
Manipulative,
Obsessed, Vindictive

FAMOUSLY SCORPIO
Hillary Clinton,
Emma Stone, Drake

Scorpio's over here playing chess while the rest of us play checkers. This smart, strategic sign has a well-earned reputation for mystery. Their still waters run deep and their quiet confidence belies an unstoppable drive. This sign gets. shit. done. And they're usually doing it in pursuit of money or power (probably both). Scorpio has all the intensity of a fire sign but with the intellect and intuition of a water sign, and that's a combination you don't want to come up against. But if they're on your side, Scorpios make committed and empathetic allies.

SCORPIO

THAT 9-TO-5 GRIND WITH SCORPIO

WORKING UNDER SCORPIO

Scorpios are serious, dedicated, and driven to succeed, which makes them prime candidates for leadership roles. This sign leads with an iron fist. Don't expect a flexible workspace or egalitarian brainstorming sessions—you do what Scorpio says or you GTFO. They're constantly cracking the whip and have some seriously high standards—they don't fuck with slackers. But they also go to bat for their employees like no other sign, demanding fair treatment and incentives for everyone who works under them. All in all, it's not a bad trade-off (if you can keep up, that is).

How to bring them your brilliant ideas

Bosses born under this sign have a lot on their minds, so they don't have the mental bandwidth for any half-cocked ideas or harebrained schemes. When you come to them, have your shit together, be brief, and then leave them the hell alone. Bugging Scorpio for a decision will just piss them off. And when they say no, they mean it. They've thought things through to the end. If you choose to challenge them, bring the facts and prepare for battle. Exchanges like that are where Scorpios come up with some of their best ideas.

How to show them your A game

Scorpio has the same unshakable confidence as Aries, but they prefer to keep theirs on the DL. And they'd prefer it if you did, too. This sign doesn't want to see any fucking showboating. They want to see you going the extra mile without being asked or promised any sort of reward. If you keep your need for praise and attention to yourself, you might actually get some. And make sure that all of your shit is aboveboard. Scorpio has some issues with paranoia, and you don't want to get on the wrong side of them.

How to keep it real

The thing that you have to remember about Scorpio (when you're quietly daydreaming about them getting hit by a bus) is that they hold themselves to the same impossible standards that make you crazy. They're not trying to be an asshole (although they sometimes succeed anyway). As long as you're direct and honest, you can probably handle anything this sign throws at you. Plus, if they see you taking personal responsibility for your work, they're more likely to focus their laser-like intensity on the slackers in the office who deserve it.

SCORPIO IN THE TRENCHES WITH YOU

When your coworker's a Scorpio, it can be hard to know what to make of them. This sign plays things close to the vest. You've probably noticed them quietly toiling away at their projects with incredible focus. You may have also noticed that "failure" isn't in their fucking vocabulary. If you can figure out how to hitch your wagon to this mysterious star, you can learn a lot from them. But if you can figure out how to complement their badass ways, you can accomplish anything.

How to get great shit done together

This sign doesn't always play well with others—they have pretty fixed ideas of how to get shit done, and those ideas don't involve other people. Let Scorpio take the lead. It's not hubris that makes them think their ways are the best ways, it's experience. They understand their limitations and abilities better than anyone. That's why you should also let them tackle the big challenges without an ounce of fucking guilt. They'll be thrilled if you take the easy stuff off their plate so they can focus.

ASKING YOUR SCORPIO BOSS A QUESTION

You: I was wondering what you thought of my proposal...

Scorpio: [Stares, emotionless, and says nothing]

You: You probably thought the projections were too low, right?

Scorpio: [Continues staring]

You: Yeah, they were too low. I'll fix it.

Scorpio: [Watches you leave, then Lysols the office]

SCORPIO

How to become work besties

Scorpios have a few more trust issues than other signs. Although they aren't quick to admit that they need other people, they do. They just want to see that you can buckle down and get stuff done without giving a shit about the spotlight. (Leos might want to sit this one out.) If you prove to them that you're someone they can count on, you can tap into some of Scorpio's best qualities—their empathy and loyalty. Then you can enjoy the deep conversations Scorpios love to have and learn what's on their overworked minds.

How to send out an SOS

Like Cancer, this sign understands people better than they understand themselves. If you're looking for a shoulder to cry on, call a Cancerian. If you're in over your head and need a fucking life raft fast, Scorpio's got you. Keep in mind, they won't help you do shit they know you're perfectly capable of doing on your own. (Yeah, they know.) And if you're asking for Scorpio's opinion (and you should, because their brain is magic), remember that they're not fucking Zoltar the Fortune Teller. They need time to carefully consider their answer.

THE SCORPIO EMPLOYEE

Scorpios are the same mysterious bastards no matter where they land on the company phone tree. These hardworking folks tend to keep to themselves, do things their own way, and accomplish amazing shit while your other employees are arguing over whether they're a Michael or a Dwight by the watercooler. Although Scorpio probably won't be team captain in the company's trust-fall exercise, they're definitely an asset to any business. You can count on Scorpio to rise to every challenge, going above and beyond what's asked of them.

How to get them motivated

You're not going to find a lot of "Jack of all trades" types born under Scorpio. To stay motivated, this sign needs a singular task to focus on—preferably one that's in their very particular wheelhouse. Don't have any fucking clue what that might be? Ask them. Scorpios know better than anyone which tasks they're best suited for. Plus, their drive to succeed at something is directly related to how much they believe in what they're doing. (And unless *you're* the fortune teller, they'll know better than you what makes them tick.)

How to light a fire under their ass

If Scorpio is dragging their feet, you probably assigned them the wrong task. (See above.) Save the multitasking for Gemini and let Scorpio play to their strengths. This is a sign of specialists—no amount of money, praise, or reward can get a Scorpio to do work that bores them to fucking tears. Helping them understand the *why* behind the *what*, however, may be the kick in the ass they need. That *why* could simply be that it's important to the company, which will tap into their sense of loyalty and their need to succeed.

How to have the hard convos

Got bad news to deliver? Get straight to the fucking point. Scorpios have no appreciation for sugarcoating and zero chill when it comes to criticism. The badasses born under this sign give their all to the job. So when they hear something's not right, they take it personally. They may even get in your face about it at first. But let them blow off some steam and they'll get around to taking responsibility for their fuckups. Just don't harp on the problem—state your case and let them fix it before getting back to doing what they do best.

LOVE, SEX, AND FOR-EV-ER WITH SCORPIO

THE SCORPIO MEET-CUTE

The air of mystery that surrounds Scorpios can make them seem sexy and intriguing. But they're not fucking Men in Black. (OK, they could be. They totally could be world-saving secret agents. That tracks.) They're usually just deeply untrusting control freaks. Scorpios need a committed relationship to bring out their best qualities, not to mention their absolutely ridiculous sexual talents. So if you're not looking for anything serious, you might want to find yourself a Gemini.

How to woo the shit out of them

Scorpios are serious people who want serious people, so impressing this sign means being respectful, responsible, honest, and trustworthy. They have no patience for bullshit or bluster. They do have the time to appreciate a well-chosen ensemble, though. Even if your Scorpio's a solid six, they expect their date to be a ten (or at least put together like one). Show this self-assured sign that you know what you bring to the table (without having to shout it from the rooftops) and you'll have them eating out of your well-manicured hand.

How to dazzle on your date

You're not going to catch Scorpio going bowling or singing a power ballad at karaoke. This sign prefers to keep things pretty chill and intimate. They love those delicious little out-of-the-way restaurants that offer unusual eats. If you really want to wow your date, take them to the little Ethiopian bistro down the street instead of the overly homogenized Italian place at the mall. They'll probably play coy and deflect your questions during dinner so they can get to know you better. That's fine for now. Just make sure dependability is a running theme in your answers.

How to cut through the bullshit

This sign is used to setting all the terms, and they need a partner who can stand up for what they want just as strongly. Bringing drama won't help you, but setting expectations with steady confidence will. Let Scorpio know that the mysterious vibe is only cute for a minute. If they want to get to know you, that shit goes both ways. But be warned: standing up to Scorpio can make them fall hard. And once they're hooked, they don't give up. You'll have to ghost if you want to shake a smitten Scorpio.

BETWEEN THE SHEETS WITH SCORPIO

If there's one thing that Scorpios are known for, it's sex. They come by that BDE honestly. This intensely sexual sign basically has the libido of a teenager and the brooding stare of a fictional heartthrob. And they have animal magnetism on lock—they're impossible to resist. But Scorpios are not your fuckbois. They take sex as seriously as work. Without commitment, connection, and discretion, you don't get to see what Scorpio is really capable of. (This might not be the number one reason to get to know Scorpio better, but it's definitely up there.)

How to whet their appetite

Scorpio could teach a fucking masterclass in the art of seduction. This sign knows how to draw shit out. They also know that good things come to those who wait and enjoy being teased as much as they enjoy teasing. Make use of all of the senses to tempt this super-sensual sign. Some might consider Scorpios a little…aggressive…in other aspects of their lives. But in bed, they're all about subtlety. (Save the groping and grabbing for an Aries.) When you get them going, buckle the fuck up!

**TOP 5 THINGS
SCORPIO DOES
TO GET READY
FOR A DATE**

1. Stalks you on social
2. Stalks you on social
3. Stalks you on social
4. Stalks you on social
5. Stalks you on social

SCORPIO

How to blow their fucking minds

Blowing Scorpio's mind starts long before the foreplay—you have to put their mind at ease first. Take the time to build up the trust between you and that shit will pay off big in bed. After that, it's all about mirroring Scorpio's passion, openness, and enthusiasm. But your job doesn't end when the sex does. Despite some serious Aries vibes, Scorpio actually *is* the shag-and-snuggle type. Be there for the spooning and deep conversation after what is sure to be an amazing fuck. (Never pass up an opportunity to build trust with this sign.)

How to get what you need

Scorpios have a sixth sense for sex. They know what you want, maybe even before you do. And they are ready, willing, and able to give it to you. Go with the flow and you might be pleasantly surprised when they hit the spot without you saying a word. But Scorpio is up for anything. Like, *anything*. Got a kink? Go for it. This is the sign to try shit with. For all of their mystery in every other aspect of their life, Scorpio is completely open and uninhibited in bed.

WITH SCORPIO FOR THE LONG HAUL

If you lock down a Scorpio, count yourself as one of the lucky few that get to see the man (or woman) behind the curtain. This sign's generous, caring, and protective side is reserved for only the most worthy. And they chose you. Don't think for a second they didn't—Scorpios don't leave shit up to fate. They carefully consider every decision, and they decided to trust you with their heart. (That's a big fucking deal.) But this sign will always suffer from some paranoia. At a certain point, you'll have to sit 'em down.

How to have a great fucking partnership

A better symbol for Scorpio might be the duck. Just below that smooth surface, these overthinkers are peddling furiously. Trust issues hit this sign hard. If you want to see all they have to offer (and you do—especially in the bedroom), you need to create an environment of trust and openness in the relationship. And when *being* trustworthy isn't enough, you just have to put that paranoid shit in its place. Tell your partner that you expect the benefit of the doubt because you've fucking earned it.

How to deal with the day-to-day shit

This super-responsible sign has no problem maintaining a home—as long as the chores list caters to their strengths, anyway. Everyone has to do crap they'd rather not do, but it's really in your best interest if Scorpio gets to pick their responsibilities. (Really, you don't want to see them try to do laundry if it's not on their radar. One wrong move and all your shit's tiny and pink. And strangely enough, they'll resent *you* for their fuckup.) They'll also need a little nook for themselves in what's sure to be a lovely home. They need a place to retreat to in order to quiet that constant hum in their head.

How to ensure you'll be a cute-AF old couple

If you're going to go the distance, you'll have to get used to Scorpio's hostile takeover of the decision making. This sign needs someone who's happy to go with the flow. And if you know how to defuse an argument, all the better. Scorpio won't start many, but you can bet your ass they'll finish them. (And when they do, they tend to Tarzan right over the fucking line.) But if you can help Scorpio live in the moment a little, you're in for a lifetime of love and loyalty.

IN THE CIRCLE OF TRUST WITH SCORPIO

SCORPIO IN YOUR SQUAD

Because Scorpios are so smart and adaptable, they have no problem making friends. And because they're loyal and protective of the people they care about, they have no problem keeping friends. The supportive folks born under this sign will always have your back (and an airtight alibi for the cops). But Scorpios call the friendship shots—and will call their friends for shots rather than any kind of emotional support. This sign tends to hit up their besties when they're ready for a good time while keeping all the crazy on lockdown. That makes them some kick-ass low-maintenance friends.

How to have a fucking blast together

According to Scorpio, that's what friends are for. These pensive people need their friends to help them get out of their own fucking heads and have a little fun. For Scorpio, a fun night out usually involves trying a new restaurant (the more expensive and unusual the food, the better). And while they want to get away from their own thoughts, they're happy for their friends to fill them with new ones. This sign loves an intellectual sparring match. But more than that, they love to see their friends having a good time.

How to get the tea

Fiercely independent Scorpio has zero interest in divulging secrets. That doesn't mean they don't need to now and then. If you want them to open up, just be patient. They'll find you when they have something to share. This sign saves the deep conversations for the chosen few—the friends who have proven themselves (and are really fucking forgiving of Scorpio's standoffish ways). And because they value privacy, Scorpio is a damn vault. You can tell them anything and know that it's going to their grave with them.

How to make things right

How do you make things right? You don't fuck with Scorpio to begin with. This sign can hold a grudge. As long as it's not a serious transgression, they can get past it and stay friends. But they'll never let that shit go completely. You can bet on some passive aggression and a few harsh remarks. And if you really fuck up? Remember the ducks. Scorpio will look you right in the face and say things are fine while secretly plotting a revenge you can't even fathom. Scorpios think carefully before they speak or act. You should, too.

SCORPIO IN THE FAMILY

Scorpios are Scorpios from the day they come into this world. Their loyalty and generosity, their jealousy and intensity—Scorpio's family gets to see it all. And family has a huge role to play in which traits win out. So, if your Scorpio kid's an asshole, look in the mirror. (Kidding—mostly.) Although it can be really fucking annoying to adhere to rules imposed by your five-year-old sibling, the feelings of trust and security you give Scorpio will last throughout their life. Treat them right and they will slay fucking dragons for you.

How to have an awesome relationship with a Scorpio parent

Even as parents, Scorpios are not to be fucked with. This sign sees their kids as a direct reflection of themselves, so they expect their offspring to act right. There are just so. many. rules. And their kids can never get away with breaking them because Scorpio has a bloodhound's nose for bullshit. That same intuition makes this sign super sensitive to their kids' needs, though. When you're recounting childhood memories with your therapist, remember to mention that your Scorpio parent also taught you how to be cool under pressure, put your best foot forward, and meet a damn goal.

WHAT TO DO WHEN YOU FUCK OVER SCORPIO

1. Have someone else taste your food

2. Make sure they walk into rooms first

3. Say hi to your new neighbors (Make sure you give them your new name.)

SCORPIO

How to raise a kick-ass Scorpio kid

At their best, Scorpio kids are smart, sympathetic, independent, and funny. Encouraging those amazing traits can help balance out the trust issues that will impact so much of their lives. But you'll need to make sure your little Scorpio feels secure and in control at home. Then teach them how to let go and forgive. Let them know that nothing bad will happen if they loosen their death grip on life. And if they can channel that focus and drive to help others, they can grow up to do incredible things. (When you want a lesson to stick, take the kid for some froyo. Food rewards are everything.)

How to go from siblings to BFFs

Scorpios will do anything for their siblings—older or younger, close or irritating pain in the ass, it doesn't matter. If you mess with their siblings, they will fucking come for you. That protective instinct might be because this is the one relationship where trust is (usually) a given. Your relationship with your Scorpio sibling can depend heavily on whether they got enough attention from your parents. (Unfair, but it is what it is.) But as long as you're kind to your sibling (and maybe let them win at Words with Friends), they'll defend you to the end.

THE LAST WORD

So yeah, Scorpios can be tricky. But you probably knew that. And it's probably why you reached for this book in the first place (along with everything Machiavelli and George R. R. Martin ever wrote). But now that you know how to handle that mysterious intensity (with the deference worthy of an iron throne), you can enjoy the best of smart, sexy, and supportive Scorpio.

Scorpio Motto

GET YOUR SHIT TOGETHER

SAGITTARIUS
The Eternal Fucking Optimist

AKA
The Archer

BIRTHDAY
November 22–December 21

SIGNS
Fire | Mutable | Masculine

RULED BY
Jupiter

ON A GOOD DAY
Funny, Adventurous,
Idealistic

ON A BAD DAY
Reckless, Impatient,
Judgmental

FAMOUSLY SAGITTARIUS
Britney Spears,
Chrissy Teigen,
DJ Khaled

You know those movies where the lead evades their would-be killer by throwing themselves off a skyscraper, revealing their base-jumping gear as they glide to safety? That's the story playing on a loop in the head of every Sagittarian. This sign's high-energy optimism and confidence can seem to border on delusion at times, but man, they pull shit off. Sagittarians want to know more, see more, and do more—they're constantly testing the boundaries of their comfort zones. And because they're so damn good at everything, they can get a little preachy with the rest of us mere mortals. But they definitely keep life interesting.

SAGITTARIUS

THAT 9-TO-5 GRIND WITH SAGITTARIUS

WORKING UNDER SAGITTARIUS

Although Sagittarians like to think they know better than anyone else, people born under this sign don't always make the best leaders. They tend to go off and do their own thing, leaving everyone else to wonder what the hell's going on. That Sagittarian independence and impatience make these folks some of the most talented entrepreneurs. But they can be hard to find in the corporate world. If you work under a rare Sagittarian boss, you can definitely benefit from their enthusiasm and self-assurance. You just might have to manage up at times.

How to bring them your brilliant ideas

Despite their lack of leadership skills, Sagittarians tend to be fair-minded bosses who encourage their staff to learn and grow. So they're all ears for great ideas. They also don't have the best attention spans, so you're going to want to keep things brief. Sagittarians need to see two things: your passion for a project and its potential payoff. Catch them right after their latest adventure (before they have time to start daydreaming about the next one) and you have a better chance of their actually hearing the words that come out of your mouth.

How to show them your A game

Sagittarians don't need to know how the chute opens. They just need to know that it does. In other words, this sign does not give a damn about details. Show them that you can get results without bogging them down in boring minutia, and you might just catch their attention. Consistently come through for them, and they may even take a small, fleeting interest in your process. This sign loves to learn new ways of doing things (on their terms). Inspire their confidence in you by being open, honest, and—most of all—brief.

How to keep it real

Don't like a decision Sagittarius makes? Give it a minute. This sign is constantly moving, thinking, and learning, so they tend to change their minds a lot. And for the same reasons, this sign needs a fucking keeper. You'll probably have to help them stay on task when they're in the office and make sure the small stuff doesn't fall through the cracks while they're off scaling Everest (literally or figuratively—you never know with Sagittarius). This optimistic sign may also overpromise and underdeliver, so you might want to help them keep that confidence in check.

SAGITTARIUS IN THE TRENCHES WITH YOU

Sagittarians make much better colleagues than bosses. This extroverted sign is a dose of sunshine in a dreary office. They not only keep things light and positive, but they also love to entertain their coworkers with stories of their adventures (some of which are even true). But Sagittarians are more than just a good time—this sign is full of cooperative, hardworking, and helpful people. And when they're not forced into corporate structure, they're pretty fucking brilliant. They just need a little help with their listening skills.

How to get great shit done together

Working with Sag is a lesson in finding ways around the rules. This sign has no time for red tape. Their independent spirit is so strong that Sag often commandeers a project entirely. (Except when they don't like it, at which point they'll just drag their fucking feet like a toddler headed for a bath.) Even when they agree to collaborate, they may walk off and chew on the problem alone for a while. Go ahead and let them tackle the big think while you work on the details. They don't have any patience for the little shit anyway.

WHAT SAG IS ACTUALLY DOING DURING THE MEETING

1. Planning a ziplining excursion in Costa Rica

2. Sending you dark memes while they "look for that file"

3. Crafting the perfect excuse for not doing what they're being told to do

4. Sleeping with their eyes open

5. Enjoying their lunch because they forgot about the fucking meeting

SAGITTARIUS

How to become work besties

Sagittarius's inexhaustible energy, impatience, and impertinence are a hell of a lot more fun in a work bestie than in a boss. (Their blunt delivery is also more enjoyable when directed at other people.) Because they consider themselves a font of knowledge and experience, they love people who are ready and willing to learn. But you also have to be ready and willing to keep shit light and break some rules to get on this sign's good side. People born in this sign encourage their work friends to be courageous and to do things their own way.

How to send out an SOS

Everyone needs a Sagittarian in their corner. Sagittarians are amazing at letting rough ideas tumble around in their heads and coming up with a shiny new perspective. And even if they can't, they'll definitely cheer you up with their sunny outlook and outlandish stories. When you ask for Sag's opinion, be prepared to hear the *whole* truth. These folks can be a little too honest at times (bordering on entirely fucking tactless). But that doesn't mean they're wrong. And if you're a friend or being mistreated, they'll use that fire to come out swinging for you.

THE SAGITTARIUS EMPLOYEE

Innovative, high-energy, productive...Sag sounds like the perfect employee. And they can be, as long as they have the freedom to do things the way they want. This sign isn't great at following orders—they usually have their own methods in mind—but you can't argue with their results. And as long as shit gets done, who cares how? Oh, you care? Then you're going to struggle with stubborn Sag. The solution is compromise. When it's important that Sag follows instructions, tell them that (and make them write shit down). When it's not important, just let it go.

How to get them motivated

The first step in getting great work from Sag is giving them a real challenge. (Don't waste this clever sign on mundane tasks or their boredom will morph into disruptive stubbornness.) Also, be very clear about the result you want and avert your eyes while they do what they need to do to make it happen. Being micromanaged kills Sagittarius's buzz, and a discouraged Sag is an unproductive Sag. But this sign is all about working smarter, not harder, so you probably don't want to see how the sausage gets made anyway. Just be happy it's off your fucking plate.

How to light a fire under their ass

You will never have to light a fire under Sag's ass—this sign's pilot light is always burning and ready for them to crank shit up to high. What you will need to do is help them stay on fucking track. The more excited Sag is about what they're doing, the more motivated they'll be to get it done. But this sign can get tunnel vision when they're elbow-deep in a project and lose track of, well, all the things. If you don't assign the little shit to someone else, it may not get done.

How to have the hard convos

Like Leos, Sagittarians are always looking on the bright side and may have no idea that bad news is coming. Come into the conversation knowing that this sign always has the best intentions. They may bend the rules, but Sagittarians hold themselves to incredibly high ethical standards. If the problem has nothing to do with them, Sag will roll up their sleeves and get to work fixing it. (So, if you're the one having a hard time, Sag should be your go-to.) But if the problem lies with them, they can get discouraged and even annoyingly mopey. Tread lightly.

SAGITTARIUS

LOVE, SEX, AND FOR-EV-ER WITH SAGITTARIUS

THE SAGITTARIUS MEET-CUTE

Look for the person lecturing their friends over what constitutes an IPA, and you've probably found yourself a Sagittarian. This sign loves to tell you things you don't know. And thanks to their thirst for knowledge, they can school you on pretty much any subject. That can get obnoxious down the line, but at first, it's fucking enchanting. Sagittarians are bright, shiny, passionate people who know how to turn on the charm. You won't have to worry about them bullshitting you, though—this sign is all about honesty and integrity. So enjoy the conversation and see where it takes you!

How to woo the shit out of them

If there were a competition for most talkative sign, Sagittarius would be tied with Gemini (which is fucking saying something—no pun intended). So give them something to talk about. Take a peek at their (probably copious number of) tweets and see if you can find some common ground. Sag wants to see your curious mind in action, so ask plenty of questions and show them you're interested in how their exceptional mind works. And if you really want to win them over, show them you know how to hold up your end of a conversation.

How to dazzle on your date

Because Sagittarians are incredibly high-energy, they don't mind getting physical on a first date. Paintball is a great option. (Get your mind out of the damn gutter. J/k—they're good with sex on the first date, too.) After you've covered your date with hot-pink paint (or whatever), pick a quiet place where you can have a long chat. Fulfilling both their physical and their intellectual needs puts you way ahead of the curve with Sagittarius. But don't pick something you hate doing just to please them—this cheerful sign is not here to hear you bitch.

How to cut through the bullshit

Self-assured Sagittarians see no reason not to be themselves at all times—for better or worse. Their optimism isn't a front. It's the root of their confidence. Sagittarians truly believe that shit will work itself out and people are generally good and lollipops grow on trees. (OK, no. They're idealists, not toddlers—most of the time.) But if you fuck with their worldview by being deceitful or disingenuous, they will drop you on your ass. This sign wants to hear about your latest adventure or how you solved a problem at work—the kinds of things that let them know who you really are.

BETWEEN THE SHEETS WITH SAGITTARIUS

This fire sign goes full tilt at everything in life, and sex is no exception. The way Sag sees it, there's no point in delaying gratification when you could be enjoying every moment. So they're not going to wait for the third date if they don't have to. (They're also not going to delay their orgasm, but at least they last long enough for multiples.) This sign knows what they like—sex that's spontaneous, passionate, and just plain fun. Leave the wine and roses, take the tequila and rope ties instead.

How to whet their appetite

For signs like Sag, the brain is an erogenous zone. You have to tease both mind and body to get them going. Luckily for you, that means that any good conversation can have a very happy ending. Start off with a little witty banter. (Keep it sexy, though. It's not a fucking Comedy Central roast.) Once you've got Sag smiling, go in with some playful touch—tickling and roughhousing can light Sag's fire in no time. Then skip right over conventional foreplay—Sag is happy to put that time to better use.

GETTING GHOSTED BY A SAGITTARIUS

@You: Hey, I haven't heard from you in a while...

@Sag: OMG hi! I actually JUST spontaneously flew to Mexico.

@You: Cool! Send me pics!

@Sag: Oh shit! Maybe! Low on data tho

@You: Oh, makes sense! Well, let me know when you're back?

@Sag: [crickets]

How to blow their fucking minds

Since all great sex with Sagittarius starts with a conversation, the first thing you need to do is get them to shut the fuck up. Just go for it—they'll catch on quickly. This sign hates routine, so flow from one position to the next. Keep them on their toes (or hands) with different places, unexpected times, new moves, and sexy underwear and they'll never be able to get enough of you. And don't forget to stroke their ego (among other things). Break out a playbook and ask them to master a pose with you.

How to get what you need

Sagittarians see no point in playing shit coy or making them intuit your needs when you can just come out and say what you want. You may as well come out with it, because you can bet your ass they're not going to mince words with you. Sex with Sag isn't a damn guessing game, it's a tennis match. They want an easy and enthusiastic give-and-take. So ask for what you want. Unless it's postcoital cuddle time—Sag won't hang around for intimacy. But you can just keep them talking and they won't fucking notice.

WITH SAGITTARIUS FOR THE LONG HAUL

Considering Sag's "rules are for other people" approach to work and life, you really shouldn't be surprised to discover that this sign isn't awesome with commitment. But they're happy to come home every night to the right partner. Want that to be you? You have to be honest with Sag at all times. (Come at them with that "lying by omission isn't lying" garbage and they will light your ass up.) And you have to be up for an adventure. All Sag wants is someone they can laugh and explore life with.

How to have a great fucking partnership
Being with a Sagittarian means keeping up with
their constant fucking movement. But if you need
a break, this independent sign is happy to explore
alone for a bit. That's why any relationship with Sag
has to be founded on trust and integrity to work. Oh,
and patience. Sagittarians can be cocky bastards
who lecture you when you're trying to vent, can need
attention while they wax poetic, and may refuse to
compromise without fucking legal arguments. Pick
your battles wisely (unless you want to hear about
why you're wrong and oat milk is superior to soy
milk for weeks on fucking end).

How to deal with the day-to-day shit
While Sag is busy conquering the world (and taking
selfies in Rio), they need someone holding down the
fort at home. And let's not pretend they're a huge
help when they *are* around. Sag will put off doing the
laundry until you're both down to your last pair of
underwear and you just say, "Fuck it" and do it your
damn self. Plus, this sign is shit with details, so you
know you'll have to handle the calendar. If that sort
of stuff gets under your skin, you might look into
hiring help. Sag can afford it.

How to ensure you'll be a cute-AF old couple
It's impossible to grow old with Sag by your side. The
curiosity, positivity, and enthusiasm this sign shares
with you will keep you young and in awe of the world
around you. (They see the best in you, too, which is
pretty fucking awesome.) Support Sag's sense of
wonder and encourage their fiery, independent spirit.
Stay up all night with them, talking and laughing.
And forgive them for being a pain-in-the-ass know-
it-all. Sagittarians may not be the most affectionate
partners, but they are a once-in-a-fucking-lifetime
romance.

SAGITTARIUS

IN THE CIRCLE OF TRUST WITH SAGITTARIUS

SAGITTARIUS IN YOUR SQUAD

Sag is the extroverted friend we all need to pull us out of our funk. They'll make you laugh, push your reluctant ass out of your comfort zone, and help you discover new opportunities. This supportive sign is always there when you need them. OK, they're *around* when you need them. They're busy people— they might not get your SOS right away. But they're happy to offer help and advice when they do. And unlike other signs, they don't give a damn whether you take it. Come at them with the same bullshit more than once, though, and you're on your own.

How to have a fucking blast together

Gee, how can you have fun with a sign that hates to be bored, loves to bend the rules, and sees the silver lining in fucking everything? Yeah, having fun with Sag isn't the hard part. Finding your passport so that you can meet them on their last-minute snorkeling trip to the Great Barrier Reef can be a little tricky, though. They always have their eye on the horizon. When Sag is home, they usually can't spare more than a couple of hours (and they'll definitely be late). But they can make those fucking hours count.

How to get the tea

The last thing that Sagittarians want is for you to know that they're not 100 percent sunshine all the damn time. Their optimism can falter, and when it does, they need their friends to help fortify it. Sagittarians spend a lot of their time hating on people who can't be happy, so it's hard for them to admit when they're down. But bottling it up can lead to legit depression. Look for Sag to use humor to hide a low mood and encourage them to open up. A trusted friend will get all the tea.

How to make things right

Sagittarians take a "Don't sweat the small stuff" approach to life. They don't take fights to heart. In fact, they'll probably start cracking jokes about the fight during the fight. But there are two ways to fuck with Sag that they won't find funny: insulting them personally or lying to their face. If you insult this sign, prepare for them to defend themselves for the rest of fucking time. Lie to them, and you'll be lucky if they let you know your fucking house is on fire. Honesty may be the one thing Sag takes seriously.

SAGITTARIUS IN THE FAMILY

These open and honest optimists help their family members see the best in each other. And despite (or maybe because of) a little FOMO, they also help you live your life to the fullest. This sign is used to standing out, but they can actually feel like the black sheep of the family. It won't stop them from being deeply protective of you, though. Embrace your Sagittarian the way they embrace the world and you'll benefit from their brightness and courage. (Not to mention the many, many opinions they're ready to share with you. You don't even have to ask!)

How to have an awesome relationship with a Sagittarius parent

Being a bit rebellious themselves, Sag parents understand that everyone needs room to run. Try to bullshit them or act unethically, though, and your ass is grounded (which is the worst punishment this freedom-loving sign can imagine). Even with little ones at home, Sagittarians can have a hard time squashing that wandering spirit of theirs. Try to forgive them for the time they missed with you and appreciate their infectious curiosity and laugher. You have to admit it—even their dad jokes are pretty great.

GIVING SAG ADVICE

You: Just leave it alone, man.

Sag: So, you're saying I should ask her what she meant.

You: That's literally the opposite—

Sag: You're totally right.

You: No—

Sag: Thanks, man! I'll let you know what she says.

How to raise a kick-ass Sagittarius kid

If your little Sagittarian is going to make it to high school alive, you're going to need to develop some chill. These kids are not easy. But they are fucking lovable. Sag kids are free-spirited adventurers from day one. They will test every boundary, challenge every assumption, and generally make your head explode on the regular. "Because I said so" is not going to work on this sign. Instead, strive to understand and appreciate why they do what they do. That's all they really want from you. (Well, that and a puppy.)

How to go from siblings to BFFs

You can breathe a sigh of relief—your relationship with your Sag sibling might actually depend on your birth order. Older ones want to protect, younger ones want to win. Either way, it's important that you let your sibling know that they're loved. When siblings get competitive instead, it can make Sag feel left out. And although they can hold a damn grudge, this sign hates to have bad blood or negativity around them. They're ready to forgive at the first sign of any effort on their sibling's part. What they want more than anything is someone to go exploring with them.

THE LAST WORD

Sagittarians have some pretty awesome superpowers (optimism, intelligence…invincibility?), but now you have one, too! OK, it's less superpower and more insider info. But, as any Sag will tell you, knowledge is power. Whether you were wondering how to get this sign to settle down or you want in on that endless optimism, you now have all the tools you need.

Sagittarius Motto

LEAP AND THE NET WILL APPEAR

CAPRICORN
Seriously Fucking Misunderstood

The Sea Goat

December 22–January 19

Earth | Cardinal | Feminine

Saturn

Responsible, Ambitious, Driven

Pessimistic, Opportunistic, Cheap

Dolly Parton, LeBron James, Jeff Bezos

Control issues? What control issues? Oh, that giant pile of control issues Capricorn stores under their bed for safekeeping because they don't trust, well, anyone. This sign's reputation for being a hard-ass workaholic is well earned. But if you don't stop to get to know the real Cap, you might miss how enterprising, kindhearted, and incredibly fucking funny they are, too. Plus, their epic dedication and discipline make them some of the best friends and partners you could ask for. If you can help Cap unclench, they may just turn out to be your favorite person.

CAPRICORN

THAT 9-TO-5 GRIND WITH CAPRICORN

WORKING UNDER CAPRICORN

You would be amazed (though not a bit fucking surprised) at how many hardworking Caps land in leadership roles. Capricorn is a cardinal sign, which means they are the HBIC. You don't question, ignore, or outshine a Cap boss. They earned their fucking spot, and they're not going to let anyone come for it. This sign also does not suffer fools. If you're going to work under Cap, you had better bring your damn A game. Those who do, get to experience Cap's sense of humor in all its sarcastic glory.

How to bring them your brilliant ideas

Caps can be so serious that they seem totally unapproachable (and just a little terrifying). But break through the barrier and you'll find some pretty warm and wonderful people. So don't be afraid to approach this sign with your ideas. Just bring the data to back your shit up—Caps don't do well with abstract concepts. Any presentation or paper should be super thorough, with every detail covered and communicated. And you have to give this sign time to think (and go over your proposal with a fucking fine-tooth comb). Intimidating? Yes. Scary? Nope.

How to show them your A game

When it comes to work habits, Caps consider imitation the best form of flattery. This sign spends their life making sure they're indispensable at work. So clock their methods. Showing them you can get shit done without prompting is the first step. (That requires some initiative, but not too much. Keep all of your thinking squarely inside the box.) If they let you have any of the decision-making responsibility, it's not just because they think you can handle it. It's because they expect you to fucking *channel them* and do what they would do.

How to keep it real

Cap bosses want to see results. They don't give a shit about how you feel or whether you're passionate about a project. You're at work, not baking pies for a small-town fair. Get. it. done. And don't even knock on their office door with a damn problem if you don't also have a solution in hand. This sign expects you to work like the grown-ass adult you claimed to be on your résumé. They want to see responsibility, practicality, and—most of all—loyalty to them and the company you both work for. (A dark sense of humor doesn't hurt, though.)

CAPRICORN IN THE TRENCHES WITH YOU

Before Caps make it to the upper rungs of the corporate ladder, they generally still have some chill. In fact, you're as likely to find your Cap coworker cracking everyone up in the breakroom as you are to find them toiling away at their desk. This surprisingly social sign loves to have fun with coworkers. But they can also compartmentalize and crank out work no matter what office drama Karen's bringing today. With that unbreakable work ethic and some solid comedy chops, Cap makes a hell of a work buddy to have on your side.

How to get great shit done together

Your life will be infinitely easier if you let Cap take the lead on partnered projects. It's not that they want to. It's that they need to, like Gordon Ramsay needs to yell at whimpering chefs who burn shallots. Caps actually love being part of a team, but only when everyone's pitching in. As good as they are at their jobs, Capricorns aren't here to do yours, too. They're the kid in class who turned in their portion of the group project and let the slackers hang. The lesson: pull your fucking weight or you're on your own.

HOW CAPRICORNS MOTIVATE THEIR EMPLOYEES

★ Starting the project for you because they're not sure how capable you are

★ Rolling up their sleeves and leading by example

★ Reminding you that this is what you're fucking paid to do

CAPRICORN

How to become work besties

Despite being well-known workaholics, Caps don't actually look for drudgery when changing jobs. They want to see coworkers enjoying each other's company. Think about it: Caps spend all of their time and energy at work. If they don't have a social life at the office, they don't fucking have one. As long as you don't bug them when they're focused on a task, Caps are happy to take a break and make fun of everyone's latest binge-watching obsession. Ask them to hit up the pub for drinks after work and you'll be their work bestie in no time.

How to send out an SOS

Capricorns are the "teach a man to fish" type, so if you ask for help with work, you better fucking need it. They're not here to coddle coworkers who are fully capable of figuring shit out. But if it's advice you're looking for, you can't do better than Cap. The warmhearted people born under this industrious sign don't get enough credit for their empathy. And because it's combined with the thoughtful and deliberate way they approach any problem, Cap's advice is always on point. They don't take that shit lightly, and they'll be honored you asked.

THE CAPRICORN EMPLOYEE

What would Capricorns do if they didn't have to work? No one knows. When this sign wins the lottery, they use the money to buy a business so they always have something to do. Not only do they love it, but they're also really fucking good at it. Caps challenge themselves and work their ambitious asses off to climb the corporate ladder. And because their self-worth is so often tied up in their professional accomplishments, they're easy to motivate. They don't do it for the accolades (looking at you, Leo). They do it for the respect.

How to get them motivated

Contributing to the company's bottom line is usually motivation enough, but it helps if Cap agrees with your logic. Let them know what's expected of them—methods and results included—and let them fire off their questions. The more questions they ask, the less they want to do this work. But Cap will usually fall into line when they're satisfied with your answers. (FYI, they'll also drag their fucking feet if they think they're more qualified than you are to be handing out the assignments. That one's going to take some soul searching on your part.)

How to light a fire under their ass

Considering that they're always the first one in and last one out (do they even have a home?), you probably won't need to bug them. But a little extra attention, respect, and gratitude from the boss can go a long way. The best way to motivate a Cap, though, is to show them *you* know your shit and you're willing to roll up your own damn sleeves for the cause. Cap will bust their ass for a boss they respect and admire, especially if they consider that person a friend. (Fuck the hierarchy—Caps are on everyone's level.)

How to have the hard convos

There are definitely times when you think of Cap as a machine. They're smart, reliable, and fucking unstoppable. But they're also pretty sensitive. Overwhelm them with too much bad news and it's like taking the Energizer out of the Bunny (which is both sad and disturbing to think about). And they do *not* take criticism well. When these workaholics get something wrong, they feel like they let everyone down. Any harsh words from you should be the dill pickle in the middle of a compliment sandwich.

CAPRICORN

133

LOVE, SEX, AND FOR-EV-ER WITH CAPRICORN

THE CAPRICORN MEET-CUTE

Your love story with Capricorn is pretty fucking unlikely to begin with "Our eyes met across a crowded room." This earth sign is too grounded and too busy thinking about work to notice you checking them out. In fact, you'll probably have to invent an excuse just to spend some time together. If you're on the hunt for a hopeless romantic, pick up a Libra. Caps are more interested in finding someone who's smart, charming, and settled. Add "delightfully sarcastic" to that list, and you may get yourself a date.

How to woo the shit out of them

Caps are serious, contemplative people who hold on to a lot of stress, and they need an outlet for all that shit. Laughter soothes their harried soul. So if you can bring the funny, you're already ahead of the curve. But combine a great sense of humor with quick thinking and common sense, and you'll have Cap wrapped around your little finger. This smart sign needs an intellectual equal, someone who can keep up with their wit and ambition. Play it cool, though—they like a little hard-to-get.

How to dazzle on your date

Unlike Scorpio, Cap isn't down for trying Peruvian food on a first date. This Saturn-ruled sign is all about comfort. So basically, don't take Cap anywhere you wouldn't take your Grandpa Joe. Dinner at a favorite neighborhood bar would do the trick, maybe following a stroll through the museum. Keep things casual, but make sure you look good. Caps have their shit together and need to know that you do, too. A curated look speaks volumes. (But you should also actually speak volumes about the many ways in which you have your shit together.)

How to cut through the bullshit

During your date, you might think that Cap is trying to impress you with all that work talk. They're not. This is who they are. If you're in this, get good with hearing about work all the fucking time. And listen carefully to the stories (instead of letting your fucking eyes glaze over). This is a great way to get a peek at who your Cap is underneath it all. Getting them to talk about anything other than work is a huge accomplishment. Getting them to bend a rule is a fucking miracle.

BETWEEN THE SHEETS WITH CAPRICORN

Capricorn might seem like the Red Room type, but they've had enough of fucking rules at work. Sex with Cap is playtime, and it's super fucking hot. If you like to take things slow, you better speak up—this sign can go from zero to sixty quick. They know exactly when they want you, how they want you, and where they want you because they've been thinking about it all fucking day. But Caps can't relinquish control entirely. To really give it their all, this sign needs to be in a stable, committed relationship.

How to whet their appetite

The best part about sex with Cap is how they let their imagination run wild. You could be sitting there having a conversation and have no idea what delicious debauchery is going through their mind. They're constantly fantasizing about what they want to do to you. So when you finally get down to it, Cap's motto is "Less talk, more action." Skip the fucking rose petals and just go for it. They won't be shy about sharing their fantasies with you.

CAPRICORN SLIDING INTO YOUR DMS

@Cap: Hey, cutie! Got room in that 5-year plan for me?

CAPRICORN

How to blow their fucking minds

Cap's engine might come with remote start, but they like to take things slow once they're in the driver's seat. In fact, they might be physically incapable of a quickie, so make sure you set aside some time. Because Caps know—in vivid fucking detail—what they want, blowing their mind is as easy as following directions. Make their fantasies come true and they'll never let you go. And make sure you keep things light and playful. Caps have enough seriousness in their life.

How to get what you need

Have fantasies of your own? This sign is all ears. Caps want to get creative in the bedroom and they like a sexy surprise. So they have no problem with you asking for what you want. And they're happy to pull an all-nighter to ensure you both thoroughly enjoy yourselves. Not only are Caps out-of-the-box thinkers between the sheets, but they're also snuggly sweethearts afterward. You'll never have a problem feeling connected to a Capricorn. (So much for that "all work" reputation, huh?)

WITH CAPRICORN FOR THE LONG HAUL

This structure-loving sign was built for relationships. And while their quiet version of romance might not make the Internet swoon, there's no mistaking the love they feel for their other half. Capricorns are the "You and me against the world" type of partner. They need an equal, someone willing to put in as much work as they will (and preferably someone who's as ambitious and successful as they are). Their gentle support might give way to outright fucking pushiness at times, but it's only because they want the best for both of you.

How to have a great fucking partnership
Because Caps are true partners, they're good with relationship maintenance. But that shit's going to be on their schedule. And don't expect to get one of those little reminder postcards in the mail. With this sign, it's like a timer goes off in their brain that lets them know it's time to talk about why you keep buying fucking grapefruit when you hate grapefruit. (It's good for you.) And you'll just have to get used to their job being a running theme in your arguments—being too busy with work is a blanket excuse for any and all Capricorn shortfalls.

How to deal with the day-to-day shit
It's one thing for a stubborn Capricorn to exercise their control issues at work, but it's a *whole* thing when you're sharing a home with that attitude. This sign likes their living-room arrangement (and everything else) just so. The good news is, they love to do chores with their partner. Something about the companionship and structure of it all appeals to them. And, of course, Cap is happy to help you succeed in your career. Just keep in mind that they're more personal trainer than life coach—there will be some pain with your gain.

How to ensure you'll be a cute-AF old couple
If you're going to make it to the porch swing with Capricorn, you need to have a sense of humor. Laughter helps Cap let go of the workday and feel close to you. And it helps you not hit them over the fucking head with a frying pan when they try to boss you around like you're one of their terrified employees. If they pull that shit, give it right back to them. They'll respect you for standing your ground (and know to shut their fucking mouth next time).

IN THE CIRCLE OF TRUST WITH CAPRICORN

CAPRICORN IN YOUR SQUAD

Capricorns' networking skills are honed, so they have no shortage of acquaintances. But they treat their short list of true friends like family. The select few get to know the supportive, loyal, trustworthy, and funny-as-hell friend Cap can be. More than anything, Caps want their friends to be happy. And they'll do whatever it takes to make that happen, even if it means leaving work. (Insert dramatic my-husband-came-back-from-the-dead soap-opera-style gasp here.) This is one sign you definitely want in your corner.

How to have a fucking blast together

You're not going to find Cap hanging from the fucking chandeliers in Vegas—this super-responsible sign is all about a relaxed hang. (And they're smart enough to know that nothing stays in Vegas when your bestie has a smartphone.) To the untrained observer, Capricorns might even seem like boring introverts. But this sign likes to have a good time. They just prefer small groups, where their quirky personality can really shine. (And where they can easily mitigate the consequences of their less-responsible friends' actions.)

How to get the tea

Capricorns have no fucking problem telling you exactly what they think, but you might want to put the tea back in the damn pot. This sign calls it like they see it. And they have set opinions on pretty much everything, which they're happy to share at frequent intervals. The thoughts you won't mind hearing usually have to do with work (surprise, surprise). Caps sound like they're doing stand-up when they vent about their coworkers' fuckups, and that's just a good time for everyone. (Well, except for the coworkers.)

How to make things right

It can be a little too easy to abuse a Capricorn's generosity and helpfulness, which are fucking limitless when it comes to close friends. Even when they start to get resentful, Cap will keep on giving you everything they have. Check in with yourself every so often to make sure you give as much as you get. (Or close to it—they set a really fucking high bar.) Caps believe that actions speak louder than words, so show your appreciation rather than just saying a quick "thanks."

CAPRICORN IN THE FAMILY

You might think that Capricorns put work above all else, but family comes first. This sign will do anything for their loved ones. And as long as they're treated with respect and kindness, they'll be able to relax their ever-furrowed brow and enjoy family time. In fact, this sign has zero problems showing up for Sunday dinners (which are basically a Venn diagram of Cap's sweet spot: family and stability). As the rock of the brood, you can count on Cap to bring everyone together.

How to have an awesome relationship with a Capricorn parent

Cap parents are both crazy protective and incredibly affectionate, which can be confusing to a kid. But they're two sides of the same coin—a limited-edition silver dollar that loves their child so much they don't know what to fucking do with themselves. This sign takes the responsibility of parenting incredibly seriously (like everything else they do, but times ten). And all you have to do to be the light of their life is respect and follow the rules. Then you get to see Cap's fun side. Rebellious kids, on the other hand, will get really familiar with "the look."

HOW A CAPRICORN REACTS TO YOU FORGETTING THEIR BIRTHDAY

[Sounds of shredder as they cut you from their will.]

How to raise a kick-ass Capricorn kid

You know a Cap kid when you see one. This is the sign of old souls, and they need to be treated accordingly. Don't question their choices or mock their seriousness. It's not a mood, it's who they are. Instead, help them balance out that gravity by giving them plenty of opportunities to be a carefree kid. But never forget who you're really dealing with—an old, cigar-smoking, stock-exchange broker in a child's body. These little smarties will play you to get what they want.

How to go from siblings to BFFs

Siblings are a Cap's first friends, and they can be their closest if everyone gets along. This sign's seriousness dissipates around brothers and sisters. They can smile, joke, have fun, and totally be themselves. And because they enjoy that closeness so much, they hate to fight or compete with their siblings. (But don't fucking test them—they'll come for you if pushed.) Help your Cap sibling get away from the desk, out of their own head, and into the moment. You'll both love the results!

THE LAST WORD

The only thing Capricorns can't control is their astrological DNA. But Caps are so much more than their meticulous disposition. Help yours mellow out and you'll see how smart, funny, and sensitive this sign can be. If you can pry Cap away from their fucking desk once in a while, they might just push you to be the best possible version of yourself.

Capricorn Motto

WORK HARD, PLAY HARD

AQUARIUS
A Good Fucking Human

The Water Bearer

January 20–February 18

Air | Fixed | Masculine

Uranus

Inventive, Open,
Forward-Thinking

Detached, Argumentative,
Temperamental

Harry Styles,
Oprah Winfrey,
Ellen DeGeneres

Are Aquarians a little quirky? Yes. Are they brilliant? Also yes. These are the dreamers of dreams, always working hard to grow and evolve and create a better world. The chatty, charming nature of this air sign comes in handy when they're gathering support for [insert cause here] and voter-registration events. Being good fucking humans doesn't mean they're compliant—this provocative sign likes to stir shit up. Maybe it's for the attention. Or maybe it's the only way to make a difference. Regardless, it's fucking effective. Give Aquarius the chance, and they'll show you a whole new world.

AQUARIUS

THAT 9-TO-5 GRIND WITH AQUARIUS

WORKING UNDER AQUARIUS

Aquarian bosses are kind of a rare creature since many spend their lives fighting the man. They also don't have a lot of interest in power or money, hate being tied down, and are a little too impulsive and impatient for most corporate gigs. But when you do find an Aquarian climbing the corporate ladder, it's usually because they believe in the work they're doing. Working for someone who encourages you to be creative and open can be incredibly rewarding. But you'll have to do your share of managing up with these eccentric employers.

How to bring them your brilliant ideas

Creating an appointment to meet with this rolling stone of a sign is pointless—they'll either cancel or ghost. And you can skip the presentation—to them, there is no meeting that shouldn't have been a fucking email. So, when you're ready to show Aquarius what you've got, catch them for a casual convo over some steel-cut oats in the breakroom. They want to see you bring some creativity and innovation to the (breakfast) table. But they run out of patience pretty fast, so keep shit brief. And don't harsh their Zen.

How to show them your A game

Aquarians have a rebellious streak a mile wide, so they respect an independent thinker. But this sign has a planet to save—they don't have time for your fucking waffling. They want their employees focused. Aquarians themselves are super decisive, but you may have no earthly idea what it is they've decided because the details are in their heads (where they will probably remain). So most of showing Aquarius your awesome skills will be figuring out what the hell they want and giving it to them. And that's no easy feat.

How to keep it real

When you work for an Aquarian, you have to be prepared for anything. They have their own way of doing shit, and it's not going to follow any sort of logic you're familiar with. Take notes when they talk because you may never get any more information than that. And be organized, because Aquarius won't be. Most of all, be on top of your shit. You never know when your whirlwind of a boss will ask you about what you're working on. (Telling them you have no fucking clue what they want from you isn't going to earn you any points.)

AQUARIUS IN THE TRENCHES WITH YOU

Working with an Aquarian is a lot more fun when your salary isn't dependent on interpreting runes to figure out what the fuck they want. Not only do these creative geniuses make teamwork bearable by pulling their own weight, but they also make *work* bearable with their sense of humor. This sign is a bright spot in a monotonous open-office plan. They can also be a giant fucking distraction because they prefer cracking jokes to following orders, so make sure you rein them in (or cut them loose) when they get a little too unruly.

How to get great shit done together

Naturally independent Aquarians might choose to work alone more often than not, but they can be a real asset when partnered up. As long as they're not forced to work with people who piss them off, that is. This sign is all about fairness (which is why you'll find them protesting against injustice in their spare time), so they'll never leave you holding the bag. They're even happy to shoulder most of the responsibility. During normal business hours, though, 'cause fairness means balance, and mama needs her R&R.

THINGS YOU'LL FIND ON AN AQUARIAN'S DESK

★ "You are a gift to humanity" coffee mug

★ Light-up essential-oil diffuser

★ Two sharpened pencils to hold up their perfect messy bun

★ Virgin-cotton cardigan with vegan-leather patches on the elbows

★ Colorful cat-butt pushpins

How to become work besties

Without their work besties, Aquarians would slowly lose their fucking minds having to work a "normal" job. The other air signs have an automatic in with their wit, smarts, charm, and quick-thinking adaptability. Aquarians want to be around people who lighten their load with laughter and fun. But because they're so often misunderstood, they also want to be around people who get them. Befriend Aquarius and not only will you have a lunch buddy, but you'll also have someone to trade memes with all day.

How to send out an SOS

Despite spending so much time in their own heads (or maybe because of it), analytical Aquarians can offer up some much-needed objectivity. And there's no need for formalities with this laid-back sign. Just peek over the cubicle wall and get straight to the point. They're happy to help if they can, but let them know you've tried your own solutions. Aquarius doesn't want to be your first line of defense after one weak-ass attempt. They only have time to help those who really need it—both at work and out in the world.

THE AQUARIUS EMPLOYEE

Creative and curious, Aquarians make wonderful employees. This innovative sign can help keep your company on the cutting edge by constantly challenge the status quo. And yeah, they can (and will) challenging your patience, too. Aquarians need to believe in what they're doing and will question every fucking step. And you'll probably be baffled by their unconventional methods and stubbornness. But if you can help them see the bigger picture, they will constantly strive to make your company better and more successful.

How to get them motivated

Despite their unconventional attitude and a distaste for authority, Aquarians are pretty good at monotonous tasks. You just need to let them take ownership of what they're doing to keep them motivated. They won't do just anything, though. You're going to have to choose a task that's tailored to them, and be specific when you explain what you want. (Maybe have them repeat it back, just to be sure they got it.) As long as they have a goal to work toward and the freedom to get there their own way, Aquarians will make you proud.

How to light a fire under their ass

When Aquarians start to slow down, remind them why their work matters—not to you or to the company, but to people. This sign is always focused on humanity first. The best motivation for an Aquarian is knowing that they're putting good out into the world or helping people in some way. When they get bogged down in the details, it can be hard for them to see the whole board. (And if you want to tap into your grandmother's guilt-tripping methods, you can tell Aquarius how others will suffer if they don't get shit done.)

How to have the hard convos

Summon your compassion when you approach kind-hearted Aquarius with criticism or bad news. The last thing you want to do is call out an Aquarius for being too quirky or unpredictable. That's part of who they are as a person, so it doesn't do any good to be an asshole about it. Instead, have a conversation and look for ways to compromise. If you come at Aquarius with logic and respect, they'll be more inclined to see things your way. If you insult them as a person, prepare for them to drag their fucking feet until you just want to scream.

LOVE, SEX, AND FOR-EV-ER ♥ WITH AQUARIUS

THE AQUARIUS MEET-CUTE

Aquarians can be a little guarded when you first meet them. (You would be, too, if people were always calling you weird.) But once this sign opens up, you'll be completely captivated by their wit, curiosity, and—yes—endearing quirkiness. These dreamers are also deep thinkers and great conversationalists. And they can be a fucking challenge to pin down, understand, and impress. As long as you're open, kind, and a fully functional human being, you've got a shot. (Aquarians don't have time for another fucking project.)

How to woo the shit out of them

As an air sign, Aquarians prioritize smart and articulate people who can hold their own in a battle of wits. They want stimulating conversation and a creative exchange of ideas. When you catch that inspired twinkle in their eye, you'll know you've got them on the hook. But don't just come at them with pub trivia. They want to see your passion and hear about the things that really matter to you. They also want to know they're not the only weirdo in the room, so show them your true self—quirks and all.

How to dazzle on your date

Aquarians march to their own damn beat, so don't expect them to go for that tried-and-true shit. Romance and quiet dinners are for other air signs (looking at you, Libra). This whimsical bunch likes to keep things light and casual, figuring that there's plenty of time to get serious later. And they love to explore, so maybe try a new vegan bistro together or meet them for a lecture at the planetarium. Just let the night take you where it may. But make sure your date's in on the decisions—Aquarians hate being told what to do.

How to cut through the bullshit

You don't have to worry about bullshit with this sign—Aquarians are unapologetically themselves. All of that (sometimes annoying) goodness? They're not faking it for the follows. They're honestly trying to make the world a better place. And they can be a little too opinionated in pursuit of that goal. If Aquarius seems distant, they're just in their own head, dreaming up solutions to the world's problems. Help them stay in the moment and you just might prove yourself worthy of their attention.

BETWEEN THE SHEETS WITH AQUARIUS

Aquarians are just as curious, adventurous, and open-minded in bed as they are pretty much everywhere else. And just like everywhere else, you're going to have to earn their attention by being respectful and understanding of who they are as a person. Help this passionate sign get out of their head and into their body and you'll have some of the hottest sex of your life. Aquarians are up for anything as long as they have the freedom to choose, and they do not shy away from their kinks.

How to whet their appetite

As with all the air signs, the way to an Aquarian's body is through their brain. Clever conversation is a huge turn-on. So is kindness. And if you can make them laugh? Well, that's the Aquarian trifecta. Once you have their attention, you can help them slow that ever-whirring mind of theirs by having them focus on the physical. Appeal to all five senses, letting them savor each sensation. But don't let shit get sappy unless you want to be laughed *at* instead of laughed *with*.

HOW AQUARIUS BROWSES THROUGH TINDER

Successful, conventionally handsome lawyer:
[swipes left]

Dark and brooding personal trainer:
[swipes left]

Husky content writer in wizarding robes:
[swipes right]

How to blow their fucking minds

Take fucking charge. Aquarians don't like to be told what to do, but decisive actions turn them on like no meek "Do you like this?" ever will. Because they spend so much time in their heads, it's a refreshing change of pace to focus on the physical. They want to enjoy the moment and not get lost in thought, which is exactly what will happen if you hesitate or hold back. Aquarius wants you to read them, explore with them, and help them discover things they don't even know they like.

How to get what you need

It's impossible to shock Aquarians, so don't be shy (which is a huge turn-off for them anyway). Confidently tell this uninhibited sign what you want. But don't try to control them into giving it to you. Try to dominate these freedom-loving folks—or even just tell them what to do—and you'll find your unsatisfied ass on the floor. Ask for what you want, and they're more than happy to give it to you. Routine is the death of the Aquarian sex drive, so they'll do anything to keep things fresh.

WITH AQUARIUS FOR THE LONG HAUL

Settling down with this decidedly unsettled sign can be a challenge. Aquarians are adaptable and ever-changing, but they're also seriously smart and analytical and therefore sure of their own mind. That can leave their partners a bit befuddled. Aquarians need someone who can just fucking roll with it— whatever "it" is. They can be the perfect match for open and polyamorous partnerships, but they're equally happy to settle down with someone (as long as that someone is unselfish, fair-minded, and caring toward others, like they are).

How to have a great fucking partnership

To have a great relationship with Aquarius, you have to understand the thin line that exists between sappiness and affection. This sign would be happy to skip V-Day, but don't even think about forgetting their birthday. And if you have to post one of those nauseating tributes on Facebook, avoid the cliché of making it all about you. Aquarians hate that. Luckily for you, though, arguments are rarely an issue because Aquarians believe that everyone is entitled to their feelings. Bring up any issues calmly and rationally, and your partner will be sure to find a compromise.

How to deal with the day-to-day shit

Day-to-day stuff in a relationship isn't just laundry, it's also your approach to life. And you can bet your ass that life with Aquarius will be untraditional. That might mean embracing the reversal of stereotypical gender roles or creative solutions to must-do chores. But it definitely means never letting shit get boring and monotonous. Aquarius won't, so make sure they're not the only one putting forth the effort to keep things interesting. (Oh, and set up a "fun fund" that they can tap into whenever the spirit moves them so they don't deplete your damn savings.)

How to ensure you'll be a cute-AF old couple

Aquarians make wonderful partners, but their need for freedom means they'll never be a codependent, PDA-loving type. If you're going to go the distance, you have to appreciate your partner for who they are and help them feel free to be themselves. Anything less than that will make them want to bolt. Aquarians have a deep-seated need to change, grow, learn, be better, and do better, and they need a partner by their side who's willing to grow with them. Be a friend first, and everything else will sort itself out.

AQUARIUS

IN THE CIRCLE OF TRUST WITH AQUARIUS

AQUARIUS IN YOUR SQUAD

Having an Aquarian in your squad is like having your own personal self-help guru who's also down to day-drink with you. Not only do these adventurous friends drag you out of your damn comfort zone, but they also help you grow, evolve, and become the person you really want to be (however often that changes). But they don't push—they just give you permission and space to do you. They're also loving and protective without being judgy, because they believe you have a right to discover life at your own pace. (Sound like an Aquarius you know? *cough* Oprah *cough.*)

How to have a fucking blast together

Optimistic and carefree Aquarians are always a good time. When you hang with this sign, you feel light as air. It helps that they legitimately don't give a fuck what others think of them. And they know how to empower you to feel the same (even if it's just for the minute before you remember that everyone and their fucking great aunt Dottie knows how to upload cell phone videos to YouTube). Any time spent with this kindhearted sign will build you up, make you laugh, and help you enjoy life to the fucking fullest.

How to get the tea

Come on. This is an air sign we're talking about. Aquarians are born communicators. Sit with one for more than 30 seconds and you're sure to hear a fucking running stream of whatever's going through their mind. You might not always know how they got from A to B, but you'll enjoy trying to figure it out. This sign has a special place in their hearts for hot takes, and they love any opportunity to offer up their opinions. But they also know when to weigh in and when to let you learn shit the hard way.

How to make things right

It's not easy to piss of an Aquarian. This kindhearted sign doesn't believe in sweating the small stuff. (They have an entire world to fix—they can't get stuck in the fucking details.) If you do manage to hit a nerve, an Aquarian will always hear you out. But you can expect a fucking therapy session about the why of whatever you've done. It's not a punishment—they really want to understand things from your perspective. Because they're just good fucking humans.

AQUARIUS IN THE FAMILY

Aquarians are the glue, the peacemakers, and the protectors of a family. They're the inspiration for finding your own voice and the reason to come together in happiness and laughter. These charming spirits can teach your family to express themselves equally, like a choir harmonizing instead of a bunch of soloists squawking. Sure, you might have to explain to your friends why your Aquarian sister got a ticket for dancing naked in the street on a rainy afternoon. But, really, it's a small sacrifice for having the transformative lightness and individuality of this sign in your family.

How to have an awesome relationship with an Aquarius parent

For an Aquarian parent, their child becomes their whole world. Kids embody the freedom, originality, and optimism that breathe life into Aquarius. And not only will they encourage those traits, but they'll also pour all of their love for people and the planet into their little ones to help them become incredible human beings. Children of Aquarians might have to live down a few embarrassing moments (OK—more than a few), but they get a unique upbringing in return. (How many other kids' parents taught them about the perils of drinking by letting them get stupid drunk with their friends?)

MAKING BAD DECISIONS AROUND AQUARIUS

You: I think I'm going to text him.

Aquarius: You should really think this through.

You: But I miss him.

Aquarius: You need to figure out who you are without him and what *you* want.

You: But I want *him.*

Aquarius: [Grabs the phone and throws it in a nearby fountain.] It's for your own good.

AQUARIUS

How to raise a kick-ass Aquarius kid

These kids march to the beat of their own drum from day one, so if you're the uptight type, you're going to have to get used to having the "weird" kid. But with that weirdness comes joy, optimism, understanding, creativity, kindness, and so many other amazing qualities. It also comes with a hefty amount of rebellion, so brace yourself for those fucking teenage years. This sign hates being told what to do. Including them in any discussion about rules and letting them know your reasoning should be enough to head off most fits. (Most. Not all.)

How to go from siblings to BFFs

Aquarians want everyone to be happy. Like, literally everyone. But their siblings' happiness may mean the most to them out of anyone. Too often, Aquarians end up feeling like the black sheep because of their quirky personalities. But a sibling can be the difference between high vibes and actual depression. Make sure you appreciate Aquarius's unique viewpoint and big heart rather than making fun of them. And carve out some time for exploring the world together. The FOMO is real for this sign—being included is everything.

THE LAST WORD

All Aquarians want in life is to be understood. And to heal all of the world's ills. And maybe some decent fucking falafel. And now, having read up on Aquarian relationships, you can help make at least one of those dreams a reality! If you can embrace their quirks and be a good fucking human, you're on the right track with free-spirited Aquarius.

Aquarius Motto

DAMN
THE MAN

PISCES

Dreamy AF

The Fish

February 19–March 20

Water | Mutable | Feminine

Neptune

Creative, Intuitive, Compassionate

Self-Indulgent, Destructive, Delusional

Rihanna, Steve Jobs, Millie Bobby Brown

Combine Cancer's intense empathy with Scorpio's spooky intuition and you've got Pisces, a sign that's basically looking down on the rest of us from another fucking realm. These sensitive souls feel all the feels, so you'll often find them retreating into their own thoughts. That tendency toward daydreaming makes Pisceans incredibly imaginative and absolute fucking masters at visualization. They see things the rest of us can't fathom, which makes them kick-ass creators, workers, friends, and partners. They just need a little help coming back to Earth sometimes. (And a little compassion, since they're basically a raw nerve.)

PISCES

THAT 9-TO-5 GRIND WITH PISCES

WORKING UNDER PISCES

Having a boss who can read you like a *Twilight* book would be pretty fucking terrifying if they weren't also the most sympathetic, understanding, and kind-hearted person on the planet. That's the line you walk with a Piscean boss. This sensitive sign tends to rely on intuition and feelings more than logic and evidence, so you might be surprised to see them at this level. But Pisceans also tend to attract money, which means you'll find more than a few in positions of power. Luckily for you, they make adaptable, imaginative, and protective bosses.

How to bring them your brilliant ideas

Pisceans have a reputation for being indecisive, but they're just super flexible. Unlike some stubborn signs, they *want* to be convinced of the best approach. So bring them your best argument and plenty of facts to back it up. This patient sign doesn't mind sitting for a long presentation as long as it's thoughtful, well put together, and aesthetically pleasing. But for a sign that feels everything, they don't show much. Don't freak out mid-proposal at the blank look on their face—you're doing fine.

How to show them your A game

For Pisceans, everything is personal—as in, *of people*. They have a dedicated line to their humanity. So, as much as they worry about the bottom line, they see people and not just cogs in a machine. They *want* you to enjoy your work, get along with your colleagues, and reach for the damn stars just because you're passionate. Showing Pisces your best work means being a team player and helping everyone get shit done together. (And not stepping on anyone's toes in the process.)

How to keep it real

If either of you is going to get anything done, Pisceans need your help staying organized and on top of their shit. (When you spend that much time in your imagination, you're bound to occasionally lose track of reality.) And your efforts won't go unnoticed or unrewarded. But don't mistake this sign's empathy and kindness for weakness. Pisces ain't no pushover—you can't manipulate them with emotions. They've been playing that game since you were in diapers and they're better at it. You'll be volunteering to work extra hours without overtime before you even know what happened.

PISCES IN THE TRENCHES WITH YOU

Unlike with most signs, Pisceans don't really change as they climb the corporate ladder. As employees, these mellow empaths are still focused on the happiness of the people around them. They want to chill with their coworkers and work as a team to create great shit. And they don't do well with pressure or conflict. But don't expect any Libra-level mediation—you'll just find Pisces curled up under their desk in the fetal position, rocking and quietly singing "You Are My Sunshine." So keep things cordial for their fucking sanity.

How to get great shit done together

Pisceans love to offer up ideas for the cause, but they prefer to do it from behind a thick, velvet curtain while you take the mic. This introverted sign is not about that spotlight, and some low-level anxiety can stop them from contributing entirely. They need you to encourage them by letting them know you respect and appreciate their unique talents and takes. Giving them the option of choosing when and how to help can also give them enough of a sense of control to contribute more substantially. Once they feel comfortable, Pisceans are a font of useful insights.

DISCIPLINE, PISCES STYLE

What you expect: An hour-long lecture about how your behavior is negatively impacting the company's performance.

What you get: A hug and a gift card for a tarot reading.

How to become work besties

Even in a drama-free office, you're bound to find a lot of emotion flowing around the place. (And what office is drama free? A home office, maybe… if you're not a Gemini.) And Pisces *feels* that. So what they really need in a work bestie is someone who can lighten the load like a damn emotional-support animal. You can be their sounding board and help resolve conflicts so they don't have to hide under their fucking desks. And if you could be their middleman sometimes so they don't have to battle their damn introversion all day, that would be awesome.

How to send out an SOS

If you're asking for help with work, Pisces will be with you as soon as they finish their own. If you're looking for advice about people, you're not going to find a better source than an empath. Pisceans know what you're feeling before you do, plus they're always tactful and never judgy. They will, however, take your emotions on as their own. (Ever heard of a sympathetic crier?) So don't abuse the privilege unless you want to see this sign ugly cry all fucking day.

THE PISCES EMPLOYEE

Imagination meets analysis in super-adaptable Pisces, and it makes them bomb AF innovators. This sign can project how ideas play out with scary accuracy. Plus, they're more concerned with the good of their team than with their own interests. Give Pisces a creative outlet or a job where their individuality is valued, and watch them do their best fucking work. Just remember this: overworking them will backfire and you'll just have a super-unproductive and pissed off Pisces on your hands.

How to get them motivated

For Pisces to get shit done, they need proper direction and encouragement. You need to nudge them toward the action you need them to take. Leave it up to them, and Pisces will get stuck in their own head with no way out. If motivation is really the issue, though, tap into their empathy. Your excitement for a project will be contagious with Pisces (as will your dread, FYI). If you're not sure you can pull off excitement, just let them know how their actions affect you, the team, and the company. They won't want to let anyone down.

How to light a fire under their ass

Pisceans are naturally subordinate workers, so just telling them what's expected of them should be enough to keep them moving toward the goal line. But if you need shit quickly, remember their empathy. They're going to respond a hell of a lot better to appreciation and encouragement than to any unnecessary roughness. And despite their humility and kindness, this sign isn't going to turn up their nose at a fat check. Financial incentives work just as well as verbal ones, but the combo is killer.

How to have the hard convos

This is one sign you don't have to worry about when it comes to bad news or criticism. (As long as you're not an asshole about it. Pisceans are just one big bruise, and it'd be a dick move to poke them.) There's zero ego here. This super-adaptable sign takes things in stride. They welcome criticism, and truly want to know how they can do better. So if you have direction to give, Pisces is happy to take it. But don't be tempted to take advantage of their self-sacrificing nature unless you want a side of resignation letter.

PISCES

LOVE, SEX, AND FOR-EV-ER WITH PISCES

THE PISCES MEET-CUTE

With an imagination like Pisces has, it's no surprise you'll usually find this sign out enjoying the arts. Introversion isn't a problem for these sweet and flirty dreamers when it comes to dating. They know just the thing to say to smooth over any awkwardness of a first meeting by tapping into their dynamic duo of empathy and intuition. With their natural optimism and idealism, you can't help but be enchanted by a Pisces. And the more they like you, the more bubbly and adorable they are (which means they can't hide how they feel about you).

How to woo the shit out of them

These hopeless romantics don't mind a little old-fashioned courting. They love to take things slow and steep in all of the delightful emotions they're feeling between the two of you. Win them over by letting them see that you're someone they can dream with. If you talk about work, steer clear of money and titles (two things this sign doesn't give two shits about). Pisces wants to hear about your creative contributions and discover the breadth of your imagination. And you get bonus points if you can read people (or at least them) like they can.

How to dazzle on your date

Impressing Pisces starts before you even pick them up. This sign appreciates style, so make sure you put a little effort into your look. Then take Pisces somewhere inspiring, where they can enjoy music or art—something the two of you can talk about. This visionary sign loves to bat around ideas and interpretations, gaining new perspectives from each person they meet. They'll be fascinated to learn what makes you tick and how your mind works, which means you'll want to carve out some quiet time for conversation.

How to cut through the bullshit

The idealism and optimism that shine out of Pisces like a bright, glowing aura of positivity are genuine. Don't burst their fucking bubble just because you've seen some things. So have they, and they're choosing to rise above it. If you can't view that as inspiring, Pisces might not be for you. This sign is looking for the real thing, someone who is honest and emotionally vulnerable. If you're not, bail now. They're too fucking intuitive for you to bullshit them.

BETWEEN THE SHEETS WITH PISCES

This sign's romanticism applies to every aspect of their life, so you can fucking bet they're going to expect a real connection in bed. Pisceans need the intimacy and affection that usually comes with a relationship—or at least the promise of one—to have really great sex. And it will be *really* great sex. This sign loves to please their lovers, and their chameleon-like adaptability makes it easy for them. They are up for anything and skilled at everything. And once you've earned their trust, they're here for as much as you can fucking handle.

How to whet their appetite

This one should be obvious to you by now—Pisceans need to be seduced. If you're going to see them naked, this sensitive sign needs romance, compliments, and encouragement. They want openness and tenderness. And foreplay. Lots of good, old-fashioned foreplay. (Some good, new-fashioned foreplay, too, if you have it.) Break out the candles, and the wine, and the jazz music, and the rose petals. And don't worry—sex with Pisces is well worth the effort. You've never experienced a mind-body connection like this.

A LOVE POEM FROM PISCES

Saw you at the bar

Writing in your dream journal

Could you be the one?

How to blow their fucking minds

With all that talk about romance, you might think Pisceans are shy and innocent. But these creative geniuses can be absolute freaks in the bedroom. If you want to make their toes curl, you have to be open to fulfilling their wild fantasies. And they don't want to have to fucking tell you to move to the right. Focus on pleasing them, paying careful attention to how they react and adjusting accordingly. If you learn to read their desires, there's no limit to what they'll do for you.

How to get what you need

Pisceans live to make others happy, so there's not a whole hell of a lot you have to do to get yours in this relationship. They want to please you—they're dying to please you—so you can just ask for what you want. But why not have a little fun with it and keep your lips sealed (so to speak) while your Piscean partner *intuits* what you want? They know how to read your mind, your facial expressions, your every muscle movement. And they can envision things you can't. Pisces may blow your mind with moves you can't even imagine.

WITH PISCES FOR THE LONG HAUL

Chalk it up to their idealism, but this sign believes in soul mates and won't fucking settle for less. And if they even think they've found "the one," they're all the way in. Like, Jane Austen–level all in. But you wouldn't want it any other way. This sign brings magic into your life. Pisceans have big dreams and love to share them with their partners. Their passion can morph into possession at times, though, so they need a little reassurance on your part when they're feeling insecure. (Contrary to what Sagittarians would have us believe, optimism and confidence are not the same thing.)

How to have a great fucking partnership

Because it's so easy for Pisceans to read the people around them, they can come to expect the same from those closest to them. But you're not a fucking mind reader, and you need to let them know that. They'll hate to burden you with their shit, but they need to—empaths need an outlet for all the emotion they absorb or they can burn out like a Motel 6 porchlight. You have to create a safe and loving environment for them to open up, and then just fucking deal with the hour-long conversation that follows.

How to deal with the day-to-day shit

With your Piscean partner's head in the clouds, you'll need to keep track of the day-to-day shit. And you may want to take over the money stuff entirely—this sign can get a little spendy with the retail therapy. Thanks to their childlike optimism, Pisceans have a tendency to think that problems will just go away on their own. But these empaths take the ups and downs of a relationship really personally and can crash and rise with them. Pick your battles carefully, and approach Pisces with the same kindness they show you every day.

How to ensure you'll be a cute-AF old couple

These dreamers will never get tired of your love story, which is how they see your relationship. Help them maintain that joyful perspective by keeping the romance alive. That's not just sweet little gestures, either. This sign needs sex and affection like they need air. (Good news for you, right?) They also need your blessing. Although Pisceans can get a little possessive of their boo, they need you to allow them the freedom to follow their bliss. Their passion and creativity depend on it. And remember, your happiness depends on theirs.

PISCES

IN THE CIRCLE OF TRUST WITH PISCES

PISCES IN YOUR SQUAD

Piscean friendships are solid AF. This deeply loyal and sympathetic sign connects with people on a level unlike anything you've experienced before. And they can't have that connection with just any fool, so count yourself lucky to be among the chosen few. Pisces will always have your back and put you above everyone else—including themselves. They'll also be honest with you when you need it most (but unlike a Capricorn, they'll do it with a little fucking tact). This sign knows exactly what to see to give you what you need.

How to have a fucking blast together

With an imagination that runs wild on the daily, this sign knows how to dream up a few thousand ways to have a good time. And they get you better than anyone else, so they'll know what you feel like doing and when you're just not into it. You'll never not have fun with Pisces. But if you want to tap into that incredible mind of theirs, get creative together. It doesn't have to be serious—a paint-and-sip party would do the trick. (Just don't let them drink too much wine or you'll have to pull them out of their feels.)

How to get the tea

Pisceans basically live in a 24-hour confessional—everyone comes to them with their shit. And they're so used to being everyone else's shoulder to cry on that they have no idea how to get what they need. But God knows they need to let it out! Let Pisces know that you're here for whatever, from a little vent session to an existential crisis. And help them sort out everyone else's emotional baggage from their own. So, basically, be like their personal baggage claim. Only with better fucking wait times.

How to make things right

If you fuck up with Pisces, plan to talk it out. Like, a lot. Really…so. much. talking. This sign is low-key terrified of conflict, so they're going to want to do everything in their power to avoid it. That means getting to know you better than your fucking therapist knows you. Pisces has no problem putting in the work to ensure that your friendship lasts. Thankfully, with their empathy always in overdrive, they have no problem seeing your side of things. And this sign is beyond happy to forgive and forget.

PISCES IN THE FAMILY

Having a Pisces in the family is awesome. Unless yours is one of those stiff-upper-lip families who don't like to talk about their feelings. Then you're a little fucked, because Pisces will have you spilling the deets on your fourth-grade crush before you can say, "I'm fine." But that same connection and compassion make Pisceans fiercely loyal and protective of the family. They want what's best for the people they love. And having a practical daydreamer in the family can come in handy. They'll encourage you to go for your dreams and see the best in any situation.

How to have an awesome relationship with a Pisces parent

Being a Piscean parent isn't easy—this nurturing and sympathetic sign feels every skinned knee and bully-induced insecurity. But they also feel every little win and inspiring discovery. And they know intuitively what their kids need, encouraging the creativity and imagination that's necessary to a happy childhood. If you have a beef with your Piscean's tendency to avoid reality, remember how awesome they were in those early days. Yes, they made you late to school occasionally (all the damn time, actually), but they filled your young mind with wonder.

HOW PISCES CHEERS YOU UP

1. Hosts a paint-your-pet party for you

2. Helps you create a new vision board

3. Takes you to have your aura cleansed

How to raise a kick-ass Pisces kid

You've always wanted a parrot who can read your thoughts, right? That's basically what it's like to have a Piscean child in the house. It's even more fun when they go to school and mimic your bad mood (plus a few select words you didn't know they caught). Although these little dreamers need help keeping their feet on the ground, their imagination is one of their greatest assets. Encourage them to open up to you with their ideas and emotions, which can be too much for them at times. (And make them understand the meaning of "stranger danger." These kids are way too fucking trusting.)

How to go from siblings to BFFs

Pisceans see siblings as built-in besties. This sign loves to reminisce about growing up and relive the memories you share (yes, even the embarrassing ones). For them, it's just another dreamscape. At some point in their lives, they're going to learn they can't trust everyone. (Hopefully, that happens before they end up with their tongue frozen to a fucking flagpole.) But Pisceans know that they can trust their siblings. And because no one knows them better, a Piscean's sibling is their best source of support. Just return their love and compassion and you'll have a lifelong connection.

THE LAST WORD

With all that intuition and empathy, Pisceans have always had a leg up on the rest of us. But no more! Armed with this insightful info, you can finally connect with Pisces on their own ethereal plane. Or at least meet somewhere in the middle. And it's really the least you can fucking do for someone who's mission in life is to make you happy.

Pisces Motto

I FEEL THAT

ABOUT THE AUTHOR

Amelia Wood is a Gemini who gets sh*t done.
When she's not staring into your soul after you've
told her your sign, she can be found multitasking
the sh*t out of writing projects and charming the
pants off all of her friends and accomplices.